DPSST
Armed Security

Instructor Zulu

This Manual Contains Graphic
Images & Topics

Table of Contents

Class Briefing..p. 7

Section 1 – General Firearms Safety......................................p. 9

Section 2 – Responsibilities of the Armed Officer....................p. 16

Section 3 – Use of Force..p. 20

Section 4 – Decision Making Responsibilities..........................p. 28

Section 5 – After Using Deadly Physical Force........................p. 34

Section 6 – Decision Making Scenarios..................................p. 37

Section 7 – Thinking About Tactics.......................................p. 46

Section 8 – Nomenclature and Inspection..p. 58

Section 9 – Care and Cleaning..p. 68

Section 10 – Low Light Shooting..p. 75

Section 11- Training For Tomorrow...p. 86

Section 12 – What is Force Science..p. 95

Section 13 - Preemptive Legal Defense..p. 107

Section 14 – Loading & Reloading..p. 110

Section 15 – Malfunction Mitigation..p. 117

Section 13 – Loading & Reloading..p. 127

Class Briefing

Class Safety Rules:

This is a 24-hour DPSST Armed Security Professional certification class, which consists of both classroom and range participation. DPSST is bound by Oregon statute and administrative rule, with give strict guidelines as to certification eligibility. For this reason, successful completion of this class can ONLY be certified if the trainee has:

1. Attended the entire class, totaling 24-training-hours. If an excusable absence does occur, it is the student's responsibility to make-up hours and sections missed, with the instructor.

2. Scores 100% on the Basic Open Book Exam.

3. Scores 100% on the Skills Texting examinations.

4. Maintained firearms safety through the entirety of the class.

ZuluSafe Range Rules:

1. We operate a 'Hot Range' meaning firearms are treated as if they are loaded at all times. Handguns shall remain holstered and long-guns slung and oriented so they are pointed down towards the ground at all times, unless otherwise instructed by the Range Master or Range Safety Officer(s).

2. All loading and unloading of firearms shall be conducting ONLY at the firing line, while under direct supervision of the Range Master or Range Safety Officer(s).

3. While re-loading and unloading firearms magazines, you will assure your handgun remains <u>holstered</u> and your long-gun is slung and oriented so that it points down towards the ground at ALL times.

4. All range firing shall be conducted under the direct supervision of the Range Master or Range Safety Officer(s).

5. When actively engaged in a course of fire, <u>KEEP FIREARMS POINTED DOWN RANGE AT ALL TIMES</u>. This course involves movement exercises and courses of fire, which place you in close and dangerous proximity to other students and staff. You shall maintain situational awareness at all times and assure you NEVER point your firearm at other students or staff members.

6. NEVER move forward of the firing line until cleared and directed to do so by the Range Master or Range Safety Officer(s). This includes the retrieval of items dropped on the deck.

7. Call out loudly if you do not understand a command. When in doubt DON'T SHOOT!

8. If you notice an unsafe or hazardous situation loudly yell "CEASEFIRE!" If a Ceasefire order is given, immediately STOP and freeze. If holding a firearm, place your trigger finger off the trigger and outside the trigger guard. Wait for further direction from the Range Master and Range Safety Officer(s).

9. Eye and hearing protection is required at all times. Due to lead exposure, wash your hands prior to eating or drinking.

Lead exposure risk:

Firearms training poses obvious risks of lead exposure. It is imperative that you take appropriate action to mitigate these risks, by thoroughly washing your hands with soap and water, prior to eating, drinking or smoking.

Assumption of Responsibility:

Firearms training poses obvious risks of serious physical injury or death. There is also an increased risk of lead exposure and hearing loss. Maintain situational awareness at all times throughout this training. Your firearm can only discharge if it is loaded and the trigger is depressed. Regardless of where your firearm is pointed, it will fire. You are solely and legally responsible for your actions before, during and following this training. Pay attention and maintain safety at ALL times.

Section 1
General Firearms Safety

Learning Goal
The student will understand his or her personal responsibility for the safe handling and use of firearms. The student will know the four Cardinal Safety Rules and understand how these rules are applied and practiced on the job, at home and on the range.

A firearm is a powerful tool that is instantly capable of causing death or serious physical injury. Like any tool the firearm has no consciousness or sense of right and wrong. It can harm both the innocent person and the wrong-doer. It is the moral duty of the user to handle, carry and use the firearm with safety and constant regard for its inherently deadly nature.

There are four *Cardinal Firearms Safety Rules* that govern the safe use of firearms at all times and in all circumstances. These rules apply wherever you may be around firearms: on the job, on the range or at home. There is not a one set of rules for the range and a separate set for the field. Failure to conscientiously follow these rules in the office, in the home or in a high risk situation can and has led to the injury and death of security officers, their family members and citizens.

All Guns Are Always Loaded

Treat all firearms, loaded and unloaded, with respect and in accord with the other Cardinal Rules. Do not fall into the trap of a "double standard" for unloaded guns. This trap waits for the officer who disregards the safety rules by allowing the muzzle to point at others or placing the finger on the trigger because he or she "knows" the gun is unloaded. You may hear such an officer say, "Don't worry. It's unloaded." You should handle any firearm on the premise that it is loaded and capable of firing. Following this rule will prevent needless tragedy and "I didn't know it was loaded" excuses. ***It is always your personal responsibility to ensure the safety of yourself and others any time you handle a firearm, even an obviously unloaded one.***

Never Allow the Muzzle to Point at Any Person or Thing You Are Not Willing to Destroy.

In order to injure, kill or damage a firearm must be pointed at a person or thing of value. Following this simple rule would eliminate the potential for killing and maiming other persons or breaking valuable property. The short length of handgun makes it easy to quickly change the direction the gun is pointing from a safe to a dangerous one. It is frequently violated when officers are moving around each other in field situations. Also, persons, who have been around firearms in a casual or uncontrolled setting, tend to be less careful about the direction the gun is pointing. Sometimes officers will rationalize violation of this rule because the firearm is not loaded. See Rule #1. Consciously and vigilantly control the direction your gun is pointing. There is no excuse.

Keep Your Finger Off the Trigger and Outside the Trigger Guard Until You Are on Target and Have Made the Decision to Shoot

This rule is critical to safe gun handling, but it is very commonly violated. Having your finger on the trigger makes you extremely likely to fire when you do not intend to. The stress of a high risk encounter, a stumble, a startle or a sympathetic reaction to the non-shooting hand can cause the trigger finger to exert enough pressure to fire. The fingers will clench when a person is startled, falls, is under extreme stress, or is fighting a threat for control of the weapon. Even under the lesser stress of range training officers will unconsciously keep their fingers on the trigger and apply substantial pressure. This is unacceptable. Many officers have injured or killed themselves and others because they did not have the training or professionalism to keep the trigger finger out of the trigger guard until they were ready to fire. Keep in mind that you could mistakenly violate the other rules, but observing this one would definitely prevent death or injury. Observing and

practicing this rule on the range is an absolute requirement to successfully pass this course.

Be Certain of Your Target, Backstop and Beyond

On the job you are responsible for every round that you fire. Even if you are firing in defense of your life, you must identify the person you are
engaging as an actual and immediate deadly threat. Just because a person is armed does not automatically make them a threat, nor does it justify shooting that person. An armed person may be a plainclothes police officer, a security officer or a citizen. It is up to you to make certain that a person is an actual threat. In the dark use your flashlight. Use a verbal challenge to help identify a questionable person.

Handgun ammunition has the ability to penetrate the exterior and interior walls of many buildings, and continue on with enough power to injure or kill. If you must shoot inside a building, do not consider walls of sheetrock, sheet metal, plywood or other common siding to be a safe backstop for your bullets. There may be innocent, unseen persons on the other side of that wall. You must know that any bullet that might miss or over penetrate will not endanger innocent, seen and unseen persons close to or directly beyond the threat. Even in a gunfight it is never acceptable to fire at motion or sound. ***Always remember, if you shoot another person accidentally, you may be charged with a crime.***

On the range every shooter is personally responsible for every round he or she fires. Do not fire until you have personally verified that you are firing on the correct target, no person is down range (forward of the firing line), and that the bullet will impact in safe containment area like an earthen berm or bullet trap. A firing range is a safe shooting environment only if every shooter takes personal responsibility for the safety of persons on the range or residing near the range. Some ranges have a low backstop, and it is not uncommon for poorly aimed bullets to travel over the top of the backstop. Such bullets will leave the range at an upward angle and have the ability to travel over one-half to one mile with enough remaining energy to wound or kill.

When you shoot, even in defense of your life, you are responsible for the safety of others. When in doubt, do not shoot!

What Is Acceptable Gun Handling?

Safe gun handling requires that the handgun should ONLY be in one of the following conditions:

Being Cleaned or Maintained

Firearms require care and cleaning. In this condition the handgun is unloaded and is under your direct control while cleaning and maintenance are carried out. If you are distracted from the cleaning/maintenance job at hand, secure the gun. Do not leave it unattended.

Holstered or Stored

The handgun is secured in a gun safe, locked case, cabinet or box. It may also be carried in a holster under your direct control.

Ready Position

The handgun is held in a low ready or SUL position in anticipation of use. The trigger finger is straight along the juncture of the frame and slide.

On Target

The sights are on a specific target and you are engaging or about to engage. If you are on target and intend to fire, (as opposed to holding a threat a gun point) your finger will be on the trigger.

Continuity of Fire

Gun handling related to keeping the handgun ready to fire (i.e. administrative loading and unloading, reloading, clearing malfunctions.)

Training

Gun handling, dry-fire practice and live-fire exercises conducted in a planned, structured and safe training environment.

What Is Not Acceptable Gun Handling?

It is never acceptable to handle a handgun in the following manner:

Dangling

You are holding the handgun in a relaxed, casual manner, and you are NOT engaged in doing any of the activities that are acceptable gun handling. If you do not have an immediate use for the handgun, put it away.

Brandishing

You are waving the handgun around or using it as a pointer. Use your fingers to point. Put the gun away.

Hollywood Ready

This ready position was a favorite on 1970's television police dramas. The pistol is held close, next to your face. This technique was only good for getting the gun in the same camera shot as the actor. In reality it blocks the shooter's peripheral vision and places the muzzle perilously close to the shooter's head. Also, it places the pistol in a very disadvantageous position should a threat attempt to take it away from the officer.

Unsecured

No firearm should be left unattended or out in the open for any reason. You have a moral and legal responsibility to maintain constant control over that weapon. If you leave a firearm unattended or unsecured, you run the risk of a child or an unauthorized person accessing it and causing themselves or others death or injury. You could be held civilly and/or criminally responsible, and you would have to live with your mistake the rest of your life.

Firearms Safety in the Home

While the four Cardinal Safety Rules certainly apply at home, firearms safety in the home will focus primarily on safe and proper storage. In your home you may not be the only person who might have access to your gun. Even if you and the members of your household are trained and responsible, neighborhood children, visitors, or relatives may have access to your gun if you keep it at home. Guns hold a powerful attraction for the curious and untrained. An unsecured gun in the home is a disaster waiting to happen, and you are personally responsible for preventing it.

You do have some options in managing this problem:

a) **Leave your gun at work with your employer.** Many employers do not allow officers to take the gun home, but others give you a choice. If you cannot safely store the gun at home, ask your employer about safe storage at work.

b) **Install a deadbolt on a closet door and routinely place the holstered gun in the locked closet as soon as you arrive home.** Only you and other responsible adults should have access to the key.

c) **Purchase a small lockable gun box or safe to which only you have the combination or key.** Again, routinely place the gun in the safe and lock it.

d) **Obtain and use a trigger lock or bore lock.** These are commonly available in sporting goods stores, and many law enforcement agencies will provide them free for the asking.

e) **Educate your family and children about gun safety to minimize their risk not only at your home, but also if they should encounter a gun while in another's home.** Children can be effectively taught gun safety if they are old enough to understand your instructions and the concept of death, and can be reasonably expected to be responsible for their actions. It will be up to you to determine if your children meet these criteria and mature enough for this level of responsibility.

Guidelines for Firearms Safety in the Home

a) *Firearms stored in the home should be unloaded, under lock and accessible only to trained responsible persons.* Ammunition should be stored separately under lock.

b) **When unloading the firearm in the home, do it routinely in a location away from family and where a negligent discharge would not harm persons or valuable property.**

c) **If a firearm is kept loaded for self-defense, it should be under lock.** A practical solution to the problem of security versus quick access is to purchase an electronic or mechanical combination lockbox, and then dry practice (with an unloaded gun) deploying the gun quickly. The added expense and effort is well worth the enhanced safety and peace of mind.

d) **If your children ask about your handgun or are curious, take the time to show them the unloaded gun and the proper way to handle it so no one is**

endangered. Many professional trainers have found that this controlled and non-mysterious introduction to firearms safety defuses much of the child's natural curiosity. Whether or not you support gun ownership, it is beneficial for children to receive instruction on what to do if they encounter an unattended gun, especially in some place other than home, like a friend's house. The answer is to get away from the gun quickly and tell an adult.

e) **Cleaning or other handling should be conducted in a place that is relatively private and free of family members and other distractions.**

f) **Keeping a firearm in a vehicle, whether locked or not, invites theft.** A reasonable solution (and often the only legal solution) is to keep the gun in a combination locked box or safe and remove it to secure storage after each day's travel.

Mental and Emotional Safety

Firearms and alcohol/drug consumption do not mix. Alcohol and drugs impair judgment, which is a critical faculty for the armed private security officer. It is irresponsible and potentially criminal to carry a firearm when under the influence of alcohol or drugs. As general guideline, the armed officer should not carry a firearm on duty within twelve hours of consuming alcohol. The armed officer should ask his or her employer for specific policy guidance in this area.

The same prohibition exists for armed officers taking prescription or over the counter medications that are labeled with warnings that advise against the operation of machinery, or carry warnings against sleepiness.

The armed officer should avoid carrying a firearm on duty when extraordinary events in his or her personal life cause the officer to experience high levels of emotional stress. This type of stress may cause the officer to be distracted or make poor use of force decisions. This is the same reasoning that recommends not driving or operating other potentially dangerous machinery when emotionally upset or distracted. The officer should contact his or her employer to discuss specific concerns.

Section 1: Review

1. What are the four Cardinal Firearms Safety Rules?

2. Who has the personal responsibility for the safety of others whenever a firearm is handled? Does it matter if the firearm is unloaded? Why not?

3. Describe what is not acceptable gun handling. Provide examples.

4. Explain why an armed officer is personally responsible for every round he or she fires.

5. Is it ever acceptable to accidentally shoot another person? What could be the consequences?

6. Describe how you currently do or plan to safely store your duty handgun. How do you (plan to) restrict access to children and unauthorized adults?

Section 2
Responsibilities of the Armed Officer

> ### *Learning Goal*
>
> *The student will understand his or her personal responsibilities and moral obligations in making deadly physical force decisions. The student will understand the importance of sound judgment in identifying and considering the use of non-deadly force options prior to using deadly force. The student will be able to identify the elements of proper preparation as an armed private security professional.*

Your initial, and perhaps most important, responsibility as an armed private security professional is to thoroughly understand the serious nature of your potential use of deadly physical force. Being armed gives you the instantaneous ability to take a human life. This is a grave and profound responsibility that is entrusted to only a relative few members of society such as law enforcement officers. The firearm that you carry has only one purpose: to defend your life or the life of another from an immediate threat of death or serious physical injury. Once you have made the decision to fire and the bullet is on its way, you cannot call it back. The results of your judgment, good or bad, will be forever, and you will be held to account for your actions.

You Must Answer These Questions:

Before (not after) you accept the responsibility of carrying a gun as an armed private security officer, you must examine the following questions and decide if you are willing to shoot and, if necessary, kill if the situation demands it. If you have doubts or a sense of indecision, then you are not prepared to carry the gun in the performance of your job.

1. Are you willing to shoot and possibly kill someone who threatens your life or the life of another person?

This decision is critical to your ability to safely and effectively carry out your role as an armed officer. You must think about and resolve this question before accepting the responsibility of carrying a gun and potentially using it. You must be willing to shoot and, if necessary, kill if the situation demands it. When the deadly confrontation occurs, it will be too late to decide whether you can or cannot shoot. Failing to make this decision now will place you and the people you work with in danger. You must decide now. Your employer cannot do it for you. Neither can family, friends or advisors. This is your decision and yours alone.

2. Are You Capable of Making an ON-THE-SPOT Decision to Use Deadly Physical Force?

Generally, life or death situations occur suddenly and do not give an officer much time to prepare or think out his or her response. You must be able to assess the situation, and make a sound, defensible decision based on the information you have at that time.

3. Do You Thoroughly Understand the Law on the Use of Deadly Physical Force?

The law allows the use of deadly force in legitimate self-defense within very strict limitations. You must study and know the legal requirements for the justifiable use of deadly force. If you do not or cannot completely understand the law, then you are not prepared to carry a gun.

4. Can You Live With Your Decision After Injuring or Killing a Person?

Your decision to shoot may have been completely justified under the law, but long after others have forgotten the incident, you will have to live with that decision. Depending on your personal belief system you may wish to seek counseling and advice on the moral implications of using deadly force to protect innocent persons.

What Are Your Responsibilities as an Armed Officer?

Continue to Seek Out & Take Effective Training

Effective training will help you clearly understand the serious nature of the use of deadly physical force, and it will help you develop sound judgment in assessing non-deadly force options that must be considered before using deadly force.

Your training will give you an understanding of the criminal and civil penalties that you may face for misusing deadly force.

Proper training will provide you with the foundation for safe and competent gun handling and marksmanship.

You Must Accept Personal Responsibility

for Your Decisions and Action

It is vital that you understand and accept personal responsibility for your use of force decisions. This responsibility demands that you thoroughly know and understand the legal limitations placed on your use of deadly force, and that you always consider what lesser alternatives or options are available before using deadly force. Law enforcement officers are frequently presented with situations that could justify the use of deadly force, but most of the time they find other, non- deadly means. Just because you CAN shoot, does not mean that you SHOULD shoot. The community and the courts will hold you strictly accountable for your decision to shoot. You must be able to explain how and why your decision was necessary and proper.

The armed private security officer has a different and more limited role than the sworn law enforcement officer. The law enforcement officer is empowered by the state to investigate crimes, make probable cause arrests, and take action to protect life and property. The law enforcement officer has a sworn duty to act when confronted with unlawful behavior or resistance to a lawful command.

In contrast, the armed private security officer is considered a private citizen, and as such has no duty to act when confronted with unlawful behavior or resistance. The armed private security officer may decide to observe and report criminal behavior rather than attempt to arrest, detain or use force.

Unless there is an immediate and unavoidable deadly threat, the armed officer should consider alternative actions like retreating to a safer position and calling for police assistance. Remember, the law may allow the use of force or deadly force in certain situations, but it is never required.

Some armed private security officers hold law enforcement commissions as full- time or reserve law enforcement officers. This law enforcement authority may not be utilized while the officer is employed as a private security officer.

You Must Be Prepared

The mere act of carrying a gun does not mean that you are properly prepared to use deadly force. Being prepared means that you have gained the mental maturity to know that the gun is not there to enhance your authority or make up for your personal insecurities. You understand that the gun is a powerful tool that can be useful in protecting you and others in life and death situations.

The gun does not make you a bigger or better person; it does require that you be a more responsible person.

1. Being prepared means that you have thought about your ability and willingness to use deadly force. It means that you have made the conscious decision that you will shoot, if necessary, to protect human life.

2. Being prepared means that you know how to make good decisions and that you will consider available alternative actions before using deadly force.

3. Being prepared means that you have invested the time and effort to gain and maintain proficiency with your handgun. There are no shortcuts to safe gun handling and accurate shooting. Carrying the gun without the ability to use it safely and effectively is irresponsible and foolhardy.

Section 2: Review

1. What critically important decision must every private security officer make before carrying a firearm on duty?

2. What questions must a private security officer answer before assuming the responsibilities that accompany carrying a gun on duty?

3. What are your responsibilities as an armed officer?

4. What is a "duty to act"? Explain how the duty to act of a sworn law enforcement officer differs compared to the actions taken by a private security officer.

Section 3
Use of Force

Learning Goal

The student will know the limitations placed on the use of physical force and deadly physical force by a private citizen or armed private security officer. The student will understand that an armed private security officer possesses no law enforcement powers, and is considered a private citizen with no duty to act when confronted by unlawful behavior. The student will understand how to avoid becoming the aggressor. The student will also understand the criminal and civil penalties associated with the misuse of deadly force.

Oregon Law

Oregon law allows a private citizen to use force in self-defense or the defense of another person. Oregon law considers the armed private security officer to be a private citizen, and therefore subject to the same limitations on the use of force, both physical and deadly. It is necessary for the armed private security professional to possess a fundamental knowledge of Oregon law concerning the use of force by private persons. **Under Oregon law the armed private security officer is NEVER REQUIRED to use force.**

Definitions

Deadly Physical Force means physical force that under the circumstances in which it is used is readily capable of causing death or serious physical injury. ORS 161.015(3)

Serious Physical Injury means physical injury which creates a substantial risk of death. ORS 161.015(8)

Reasonably believes... means that the person carrying out the force is acting on knowledge that he or she believes at that time to be true, and that an ordinary and reasonable person (i.e. a juror) would also believe to be true under the circumstances.

Statutes

An armed private security officer may be justified in using physical force during the confrontation or apprehension of a suspect, or in responding to an attack. Oregon law allows the use of necessary physical force in such circumstances, but generally deadly physical force is not permitted except as a last resort and only to protect human life.

161.209 Use of physical force in defense of a person. Except as provided in ORS 161.215 and ORS 161.219, a person is justified in using physical force upon another person for self-defense or to defend a third person from what the person reasonably believes to be the use or imminent use of unlawful physical force, and the person may use a degree of force which the person reasonably believes to be necessary for the purpose.

What does ORS 161.209 mean?

It means that a private citizen can use reasonable physical force (less than deadly force) to defend him or herself from an attacker who is using physical force.

1. Physical force is force that is not likely to result in death or serious physical injury. Generally, this would mean an attack with empty hands or no weapons involved.

2. The private citizen or armed private security officer could respond by using reasonable force such as defensive tactics controls, a chemical weapon like Cap-Stun ™, an electronic weapon or stun gun, or a baton.

3. Physical force is also reasonable if it is the minimum degree of force necessary to cause the threat to stop the attack or be placed under physical control.

It is very important to understand that Oregon law places restrictions on the use of
DEADLY PHYSICAL FORCE

ORS 161.219(3) states that a person is not justified in using deadly physical force upon another person unless the person reasonably believes that the other person is using or about to use deadly physical force against a person.

What does ORS 161.219(3) mean?

1. It means that you may use deadly force (i.e. a firearm) only if you reasonably believe that another person is using or about to use deadly force against you.

2. It means that you must base your belief on the knowledge you possess at the time of the attack, and that such knowledge would lead a reasonable person to the same conclusion.

3. It means that your use of deadly force is justified only as long as the attacker is using or about to use deadly force against you. Once the attacker stops using deadly force, you must stop using deadly force.

DPSST recommends that private security officers use deadly physical force only:

1. **In defense of the officer's own life** (to prevent someone from causing death or serious physical injury to the officer.)

2. **In the defense of another person's life** (to prevent someone from seriously injuring or killing another person in the officer's presence.

It is very important to understand that deadly physical force (using a firearm or other deadly weapon) is NOT justified to stop a suspect who is running away from you, attempting to steal or destroy property, or disobeying an order.

Becoming the Aggressor

You become the aggressor when you use force that is not justified in the first place, or after there is no longer a need to use previously justifiable force. Oregon law provides no defense or justification for the use of force by the aggressor.

ORS 161.215 states that a person is not justified in using physical force in self-defense if:

The person using the force provokes the use of unlawful physical force by another person with the intent to cause death or physical injury to that person; or

The person is the initial aggressor, (except that the use of physical force upon another person under such circumstances is justifiable if the initial aggressor withdraws from the encounter and effectively communicates to the other person the intent to do so, but the latter nevertheless continues or threatens to continue the use of unlawful physical force.)

This means that you are NOT justified in using physical force if you provoke a fight, or start a fight, or continue a fight when the circumstances do not justify the use of force.

For example, if a private security officer teases or taunts a trespasser into fighting, then the use of force by the officer is not justified.

In another example where a person attacks an officer, if that person stops using force, retreats or surrenders, but the officer continues to use force against that person, then the officer's use of force from that point forward is not justified. At that point the private security officer is using force unlawfully and has become the ***AGGRESSOR.***

Being the AGGRESSOR means using EXCESSIVE or UNJUSTIFIED FORCE

How Do You Avoid Using Excessive or Unjustified Force?

The armed private security officer can avoid becoming the aggressor in a use of force situation by:

1. Knowing when it is lawful and proper to use force.

2. Considering and, if possible, using alternatives to the use of force.

3. Using only the degree of force necessary to stop the attack or control the threat.

4. Reducing the level of force if the threat stops using force, retreats or surrenders.

5. Understanding the *Determination of Force Matrix* and using it to help make sound, defensible use of force decisions.

The Determination of Force Matrix

The ***Determination of Force Matrix*** is a conceptual model that helps private security officers understand what the proper level of force or alternate action should be in response to an attack or in trying to overcome resistance. It is also helpful in avoiding becoming the aggressor.

The ***Determination of Force Matrix*** is often expressed as a chart that shows the level of resistance by the threat, from low to high, and the corresponding level of appropriate force or action by the officer. At the lowest level of resistance, the threat may refuse to comply or offer verbal resistance. The officer would reasonably respond by calmly talking to the threat, getting information, asking the threat to comply, providing choices, and calling for assistance.

Maybe the threat resists by punching, kicking or attempting to escape. The officer could reasonably defend him or herself by using non-lethal techniques: restraining techniques, pepper spray or impact weapons. If the threat's resistance is lethal (uses a firearm or other lethal weapon like a knife or club, uses a non-lethal weapon or any object in a lethal manner, or attempts to disarm the officer), then the officer could reasonably respond with deadly force.

The ***Matrix*** also allows downward movement. As the officer gains control and/or compliance and the threat reduces or stops using force, then the officer's level of force is reduced to a level appropriate to maintain control over the threat.

Always keep in mind that your primary goal in a violent or potentially violent situation is to defend yourself or other persons from the threat.

Oregon Department of Public Safety Standards and Training
ARMED PRIVATE SECURITY PROFESSIONAL

Determination of Force Matrix	
Resistance - What the Treat Does	*Response - The Officer's Force options* (*Officer has no legal duty to take action)
Presence Resistive Presence Verbal Resistance Refusing to Comply	**Presence** Communicating Gathering Information Verbal Requests – Persuasion Giving Choices and/or Setting Limits Giving Directions Verbal Warnings **(Or may retreat if safe and practical)**
Resistance **Static Resistance** Refuses to Leave Balks/Dead Weight **Active Resistance** Struggles/Pulls away Attempts to Escape	**Physical Control** Defensive Tactics Restraining Techniques Pepper Spray **(Or may retreat if safe and practical)**
Non-Lethal Attack **Ominous Resistance** Physical Assault Punches, Kicks, Bites Throws Object Wrestles Bear Hugs Holds Down	**Serious Physical Control** Defensive Tactics Restraining Techniques Punches, Kicks Focused Blows Pepper Spray Impact Weapons Electronic/Stun Weapons **(Or may retreat if safe and practical)**
Lethal Attack - Attack with any object or weapon used in a lethal manner - Attack with unarmed force likely to cause death or serious physical injury - Attempt to Disarm Officer - Attack with a dangerous weapon, deadly weapon or firearm	**Deadly Physical Force** - Force using any object or weapon used in a lethal manner - Unarmed force likely to cause death or serious physical injury - Firearms **(Or may retreat if safe and practical)**

04-2008

and/or control the situation. You, as a private security officer, will need to use enough force to stop or control the threat. You should not try to equally match your force to the threat's resistance. You should use just enough greater force than the threat, but not deadly force.

Example: You confront a recently fired employee in your client's place of business. You ask this person to leave, but he refuses. You call for police assistance, and you continue to talk and attempt to gain compliance. After you have talked to this person for several minutes, he finally complies and leaves the premises.

You have responded to this person's low level of resistance with a correspondingly low response on the Matrix: being present in uniform, asking for compliance, giving direction, and getting help on the way.

Example: Now let's take the same situation, but when you initially confront this person, he attacks you with punches and kicks. It is not possible to respond effectively with presence and verbal requests. You should immediately move to an appropriately higher level of force. You respond with force greater than his, but less than deadly force. Such force may include (but is not limited to) pepper spray, defensive tactics control techniques or impact weapons.

If he stops the attack and backs away, you would properly reduce your force to a level that allows you to maintain control or keep the threat away from you. For instance, if you opted to use pepper spray, you would stop spraying, but you would be ready to use it again if the threat resumed his attack.

Example: Let's look at this same situation again. In this case you confront the person, but before you can say anything, he draws a handgun from under his jacket and points it at you. It would be reasonable for you to believe that you are in immediate danger of death or serious physical injury. Your response is to move immediately to deadly force on the Matrix. You would not be required to attempt to stop his attack at a lower level on the Matrix.

Criminal Penalties for Unlawful Use of Force

It is a criminal act to use physical force or deadly physical force without justification. **Even if you are justified in using deadly physical force to defend your life, you may be prosecuted (and/or held civilly liable) if you injure or kill innocent persons.** The armed private security officer who uses deadly force, or threatens to use deadly force when it is not justified or, if justified, endangers or harms innocent persons, may be prosecuted and convicted of the following crimes:

Menacing (ORS 163.190): A person commits the crime of menacing if by word or conduct the person intentionally attempts to place another person in fear of imminent serious physical injury. Menacing is a Class A Misdemeanor punishable by up to one year incarceration.

For example, if an armed private security officer, who is not acting in justifiable self-defense, draws or points a firearm at another person and threatens to shoot or kill that person, the officer may be charged with the crime of menacing.

Recklessly Endangering (ORS 163.195): A person commits the crime of recklessly endangering another person if the person recklessly engages in conduct which creates a substantial risk of serious physical injury to another person. Recklessly endangering another person is a Class A Misdemeanor punishable by up to one year incarceration.

An example of Recklessly Endangering is an armed private security officer firing at a threat (with or without justification) with an innocent person in the line of fire or in dangerously close proximity to the threat. The innocent person does not have to be killed or injured to complete the crime. If an innocent person is hit by the officer's gunfire, then the crime could elevate to criminal homicide or felony assault.

Pointing a firearm at another (ORS 166.190): Any person over the age of 12, who, with or without malice, purposely points or aims any loaded or empty pistol, gun, revolver, or other firearm at or toward another person within range of the firearm, except in self-defense, commits the crime of pointing a firearm at another. Pointing a firearm at another is an Unclassified Misdemeanor.

Assault in the First Degree (163.185): A person commits assault in the first degree if the person intentionally causes serious physical injury to another by means of a deadly or dangerous weapon. Assault in the first degree is a Class A felony punishable by twenty years in prison.

Criminal Homicide (ORS 163.005): A person commits criminal homicide if, without justification or excuse, the person intentionally, knowingly, recklessly or with criminal negligence causes the death of another human being.

Types of Criminal Homicide

1. **MURDER (ORS 163.095):** Person acts **intentionally** (has a conscious objective). Murder is an unclassified felony punishable by life imprisonment.

2. **MANSLAUGHTER II (ORS 163.125):** Person acts **recklessly** (is aware of and consciously disregards a substantial and unjustifiable risk). Manslaughter II is a Class B felony punishable by up to 10-years imprisonment.

3. **CRIMINALLY NEGLIGENT HOMICIDE (ORS 163.145):** Person acts with **criminal negligence** (fails to be aware of a substantial and unjustifiable risk). Criminally Negligent Homicide is a Class C felony punishable by up to 5-years imprisonment.

Civil Penalties for Use of Deadly Physical Force

Even if you are justified in using physical force or deadly force to defend yourself or another person, you and your employer may be sued in civil court for damages by the person or family of the person you used force against.

The person suing (plaintiff) must establish by the preponderance of the evidence that he or she was harmed; that you were the cause of the harm, and that you acted recklessly and outside the law. Civil liability exists whether or not you were convicted of a crime.

Your defense is usually based on facts surrounding your decision to use deadly force: the plaintiff's actions placed you in fear for your life or another's life; you acted within the law and in defense of yourself or another person.

Before you begin employment as an armed private security officer, you may wish to meet with your employer and discuss how you will be defended against lawsuits, who pays for your defense, and how judgments entered against you will be paid.

Section 3: Review

1. A private security officer is, under Oregon law, never required to use force. Why?

2. Explain the difference between physical force and deadly physical force.

3. Explain the difference between how a private citizen and a private security officer may use deadly force in self-defense.

4. ORS 161.219(3) allows a private citizen to use deadly physical force in self-defense. How does this statute restrict the use of deadly force by private citizens?

5. May a private security officer ever use deadly physical force to stop a suspect who is running away, who is stealing or destroying property, or who is failing to obey an order? Why?

6. How can a private security officer become the aggressor when using force? How can the officer avoid becoming the aggressor?

7. If a private security officer must use deadly physical force (i.e. gun fire) to defend his or her life, what are the officer's responsibilities to nearby innocent persons?

8. Could an officer be prosecuted for injuring or killing an innocent person while shooting at a deadly threat?

9. Name three types of criminal homicide.

10. Armed Officer's Training Manual

Section 4
Decision Making Responsibilities

Learning Goal
The student will understand that legally and morally justifiable use of deadly force decisions must be made instantly and correctly taking many factors into consideration. The student will understand that legally and morally justifiable shooting decisions require that the armed private security professional devote prior thought, study and decision-making practice.

The Decision-Making Process

Most everyday job-related decisions, both great and small, are made by understanding your private security mission, obtaining information, reviewing past experience, comparing options and alternatives, and then using this input to choose a course of action. The process for making use of deadly force decisions is similar, but the stakes are much higher.

Understand the Armed Mission

Effective protection of the client requires the armed private security officer to observe, report and coordinate assistance. The armed officer has no statutory duty to protect by direct intervention, and, in any case, that is not the reason why the officer is armed. The armed officer carries the gun because a threat may perceive the officer to stand between him and the threat's objectives (access to the site, theft, escape), and is willing to attack and kill the officer. Also, carrying out the responsibilities of observing and reporting may place the officer in harm's way. The gun is a deterrent to the threat, and a ready means of self-defense.

Know the Facts

Beyond knowing that you are dealing with a potentially dangerous person, the actual facts surrounding the encounter may be unclear or confusing. Most use of force incidents share this characteristic. You may not immediately realize that you are under attack. Your initial contact with the threat may seem routine and innocuous. Since weapons may not be readily visible or may be purposely concealed, the threat may be difficult to identify as a dangerous person. This scarcity of hard facts will require that you be aware and constantly working to gain more information to clarify the situation.

Obtain Information

You must be able to identify the threat as a danger to you or another person. This is straight forward when the person produces a gun and points it at you.

But what if a third person tells you someone is armed and threatening to do harm? Deadly force cannot be justified using second hand information. You need to see that the person is actually a deadly threat.

To help you identify a person as a deadly threat, you must ask and answer these questions

1. Is the threat armed?
2. Could the threat be armed?
3. What kind of weapon?
4. What is the threat doing?
5. Is the threat endangering innocent persons?
6. Has the threat harmed, or is the threat about to harm innocent persons?

Review Past Experience

Reviewing your past experiences and/or training is vital in making sound deadly force decisions. Ask yourself if this current situation is similar to situations you have handled before, or discussed and practiced in training. How did you respond and handle those situations? Were you able to use alternative actions, or did you have to use deadly force?

Understand MEANS, OPPORTUNITY and INTENT

These three requirements, MEANS, OPPORTUNITY and INTENT, MUST be met to justify the use of deadly physical force. All three requirements must exist at the same time.

1. The MEANS exist for person to cause you or another person serious physical injury or death.

   This usually means that the person has a weapon. The weapon could be a gun, a knife, a club, a piece of pipe, or a wood 2X4. However, some people have the strength or ability to injure you with their hands and feet. Multiple unarmed attackers may be able to overwhelm your defense and seriously injure or kill you. You must realistically assess your physical ability to defend against a larger, better trained (martial arts) or younger opponent.

2. The OPPORTUNITY exists for another person to cause you or another person serious physical injury or death.

   Is this person in a location, position or at a distance that will permit him to harm you or another person? A man armed with a knife is not an imminent threat when he is 100 yards away, but if he approaches within twenty feet, he will be able to attack and kill you within two seconds. At 100 yards this man does not have the opportunity to harm even though he has the means (the knife). At twenty feet he does have the opportunity because he could carry out an attack before you could respond. A person armed with a firearm may be a deadly threat at a great distance. He would not need to get close to cause you serious physical injury or death.

3. You reasonably believe that a person has the INTENT to seriously injure or kill you or another.

   This means that this person's actions are directed at you or another in such a way that leads you to believe that the person may inflict serious physical injury or death. For instance, a man, walking toward you carrying a shotgun, has a weapon (MEANS), is within 20 yards and can see you (OPPORTUNITY). However, unless he points the shotgun at you, and unless you reasonably believe that he intends to do you harm (i.e. threatens to kill you), INTENT does not exist. Assessing the totality of circumstances will help you determine if INTENT exists. Let's say that you are on duty at a plant, and you observe an employee take a shotgun from the trunk of his car. The employee may be simply transferring it to a friend's car for an after-work trip to the range. Or, he may be heading into the plant to seek revenge for losing his job. You must evaluate the totality of all the circumstances and actions, as well as the employee's demeanor and response to your questions or commands. All of these factors will help you determine if this person intends to place you or another in jeopardy.

Consider the Totality of the Circumstances

In addition to **MEANS, OPPORTUNITY** and **INTENT** the decision to use force is influenced by one or more factors that a reasonable person must consider. Every use of force situation is different, and these influencing factors will vary from one incident to another. Factors can combine to place you in a disadvantageous position that may require increased force. Other factors may indicate the use of lesser force or taking alternative action if circumstances are weighted in your favor (e.g. a small sixty-year-old woman punches a fit, thirty-year-old officer).

1. Is there an age difference between you and the threat that would place you at a disadvantage? A teenager has about twice the stamina of a middle aged person.

2. Is the threat clearly bigger and stronger than you?

3. Is there a difference in physical fitness between you and the threat?

4. Does the threat display or use martial arts skills?

5. Are you out-numbered? Is there one of you and four of them?

6. Does the threat have immediate access to a weapon like a knife or gun? Are there common items that could be used as a weapon? This factor is a very serious concern in your use of force decision.

7. Who has the high ground or position of advantage?

8. Do you have cover available?

9. Is there an obstacle between you and the threat?

10. Do you have a clear path of retreat?

11. Do you or the threat possess any special knowledge that would give one of you an advantage? Do you know this particular threat? Does he usually carry a weapon? Does he have a history of violence?

12. If you are hurt or exhausted, how much longer can you defend yourself? Are you able to summon assistance from law enforcement or other security officers? How long will it take for them to arrive?

13. Does the threat appear or act intoxicated? Alcohol and drugs may alter a person's perceptions and judgment. Some drugs may give a person a boost in physical strength.

14. If you are not able to stop or control the threat, who may be injured by the threats actions?

It is reasonable that a disparity in age, fitness, gender, physical size or skill level may require that an officer use more or less force to control a situation or defend against an attacker. It is reasonable that a single security officer without back-up may have to use more force to defend against multiple threats.

Give the Threat Clear, Understandable Commands

Does the threat understand who you are and what you want him to do? In some instances, you may have the opportunity to de-escalate a potentially deadly situation by giving clear verbal commands. Identify yourself. It is not reasonable to expect that someone will follow your orders if you are not in uniform or they cannot see who you are. The proper form of self-identification is a matter of your employer's policy, but here are some choices:

- "Security Officer"
- "Security"
- "Private Security"
- "Armed Security"

You **MAY NOT** identify yourself as a law enforcement officer, police officer, peace officer, public safety officer or deputy sheriff. When working for a private employer, even if you hold a reserve police officer commission, or you are deputized by the county sheriff, you must identify yourself as a private security officer.

If the person is moving or attempting to escape, the proper commands include **"STOP!"** or **"DON'T MOVE!"** If the person continues to move away, you MAY NOT use deadly physical force.

If a person is threatening you with deadly force, and you have time, you must issue a command like:

- "Stop or I'll shoot."
- "Drop the gun/knife/weapon, or I'll shoot."

If the threat is immediate, and you are in the process of defending yourself, you do not have to issue a command. Your commands must be clear and repeated until the threat complies. Avoid the use of profanity and slang terms like "freeze".

Examine Alternatives to Force

1. Is this use of force worth the risk of injury to yourself or the threat?

2. Is there anything you can do now to safely de-escalate the situation or break contact with the threat?

3. Is this the reasonable amount of force necessary to control the threat?

4. Does the threat have the opportunity to comply with your commands?

5. Is force, physical or deadly, your only option, or can you take another action without placing yourself at unacceptable risk?

Section 4: Review

1. Explain the meaning of MEANS, OPPORTUNITY and INTENT. Provide an example of each.

2. Describe some of the factors that must be taken into consideration when considering the totality of the circumstances.

3. Give an example of the voice commands you would use to confront an armed threat.

4. What are some of the alternatives to force that an armed officer should consider?

Section 5
After Using
Deadly Physical Force

> ### *Learning Goal*
>
> *The student will understand the need for caution in dealing with the threat, responding law enforcement and by-standers after a use of deadly force encounter. The student will be aware that he or she may experience a wide range of emotional and perceptual responses after a life or death confrontation.*

The Immediate Aftermath

The immediate aftermath of a self-defense shooting can be chaotic and emotionally confusing if the armed private security professional has not given thought to his or her response. You should expect and be ready to encounter a bleeding, and, perhaps, dying threat, distraught by-standers, shouted accusations and witnesses. Due to your natural survival response you may not remember firing your weapon or hearing its report. You may be experiencing "tunnel vision" in which your senses and thoughts focus solely on the threat to the exclusion of other activity around you. You may feel elated to have survived and, at the same time, guilty for harming another human being. Law enforcement psychologists know that these reactions are normal and to be expected.

Always remember that this immediate aftermath is a very dangerous time. The threat may not be out of the fight and could still pose a danger to you and others. You may be wounded, but you should be mentally prepared to remain alert and in readiness to continue the fight if necessary. Additional unidentified threats may be a danger, and you must be looking for them and ready to engage if needed.

- 34 -

Recommended Post-Shooting Actions

Think about the following recommended post-shooting responses and visualize yourself carrying them out in a calm and professional manner.

1. **Get behind cover and observe the threat until you are reasonably certain that the threat is no longer a danger.** A weapon in the threat's hand would be an indicator that he or she may still be capable of harming you or another person.

2. Once you have established that your attacker is no longer a threat, summon medical assistance and administer first aid within your training and ability. Be aware of blood-borne hazards.

3. Notify law enforcement (911) immediately. The police will be responding to a "shots fired" call. You should expect them to be very cautious and to approach with weapons drawn and ready. The police will not know who you are, or which side you are on. A mistaken identity shooting is a real possibility if precautions are not taken. This caution is especially critical in plain-clothes assignments.

4. If possible, holster your weapon when the police arrive on the scene. Under no circumstances should you turn or otherwise point your gun in the direction of the responding officers. **Keep your hands clearly away from your holstered gun. This is especially important if you are not in uniform. Your identification should be in your hand displayed palm out. Always follow the orders of the police even if that means submitting to a high risk procedure (being prone out and handcuffed). The main goal is to stay calm, to make no suspicious or sudden movements, and let the police sort out the situation.**

5. Cooperate with the police, but remember that you do not have to talk to them or give a statement without an attorney's advice. If you choose to not answer questions or give a statement, be prepared to be detained or arrested based on the information that the police officers have at that time. Be as calm as possible and do not resist.

6. Be prepared to surrender your weapon and other personal items including clothing. Before you begin work as an armed officer, you may wish to speak with your employer about what legal assistance will be provided to you in the event of a shooting. You should also ask about the availability of counseling to help you deal with your emotions and perceptions following a deadly force encounter. A skilled counselor can help you understand your reactions, and help you reconcile negative thoughts or feelings. It would be a good idea to see a counselor whether your employer provides one or not.

Section 5: Review

1. What are the priority post-shooting actions the private security officer should take?

2. What should the private security officer do with his or her firearm before the police arrive on the scene? What should the private security officer never do with the firearm as the police arrive on the scene?

3. Describe how the private security officer, who has just used deadly force, should interact with the police.

Section 6
Decision Making Scenarios

Learning Goal
The student will practice decision-making by reading the following scenarios and writing a brief description of how the student would respond and why. The student will develop a basic understanding of how to apply the decision- making process to potentially deadly force situations.

The scenarios that follow may be typical of those you encounter on the job in real life. Project yourself into each scenario and in the space allowed write a description of the proper action or response you would take and why you would take it. In each scenario make the decision to shoot or not shoot.

Scenario #1

You are a lone armed security officer patrolling a warehouse on the night shift. The warehouse is located in an industrial area, and it contains electronic equipment including televisions and stereos. It is 3:00 AM when you hear noises in an area of the warehouse and you move to investigate. You approach the area cautiously and observe two men stacking cartons near a door. The door appears to have been forced open. Both men hear you approach and turn toward you. Their hands are empty and they do not move in your direction.

What is your response?

Why?

Is there a better course of action?

What are your alternatives?

Scenario #2

You are an armed plainclothes security officer in a department store. You have followed a suspicious acting woman in the store for about ten minutes, and during that time you have observed her place several items of merchandise in her large purse. She passes the check stand without paying and quickly walks toward the parking lot. Just outside the store you identify yourself and ask her accompany you back into the store. She refuses and continues to walk away. You identify yourself again and indicate that you are placing her under citizen's arrest for shoplifting and that she must await the arrival of the police. She ignores you, and you place a hand on her arm to detain her. At this point the shoplifting suspect attacks you with her hands, striking and scratching you in the face. The suspect then turns and runs away. You order her to stop, but she continues to flee.

What is your response?

Why?

Is there a better course of action?

What are your alternatives?

Scenario #3

You are an armed private security officer on your way home from work. You are still in uniform and you have your duty belt and weapon on. It is 1:00 AM, and you decide to stop at the all-night market for a deli sandwich. As you park your car, two masked men back out of the store with guns in their hands. The store is well lighted, and you can see the clerk behind the counter with her hands high in the air. You do not have a radio or cell phone with which to call for help. The gunmen see you, turn and point their guns toward you.

What is your response?

Why?

Is there a better course of action?

What are your alternatives?

Scenario #4

You are an armed armored truck security officer delivering cash to a store in a busy shopping mall during business hours. As you and your partner officer carry the cash to the store entrance, a man steps out of a store as you walk by and pulls a baseball bat from under his coat. He hits your partner in the head, knocking him to the ground. You have the cash bag in hand as the man now turns toward you ready to swing the bat.

What is your response?

Why?

Is there a better course of action?

What are your alternatives?

Scenario #5

You are an armed security officer assigned to guard a bank lobby. In the event of a robbery your post orders are to trip the alarm if possible, and not attempt to apprehend or engage any robbers. You notice that one of the tellers is glancing toward you and he looks frightened. A customer is standing at his window. As you move toward the teller to determine the problem, the customer turns, and you see him reach under his jacket as if drawing a gun. At this point you are standing five feet from the threat.

What is your response?

Why?

Is there a better course of action?

What are your alternatives?

Scenario #6

You are an armed security officer assigned to guard the main gate at a storage facility. Your job is to identify people and vehicles going in and out of the gate. Your orders include denying access to unauthorized persons. A car has pulled up to the gate, and the driver is unable to show the proper identification or give you a good reason to allow entry. You refuse this person entry and have not opened the gate. You order the driver to leave.

The car begins to back away, but the driver suddenly shifts into low gear and rams the gate, which partially opens. The driver backs the car and turns the wheels in your direction and accelerates at you. Your only protection is the sheet metal guard shack.

What is your response?

Why?

Is there a better course of action?

What are your alternatives?

Scenario #7

You are an armed and uniformed security officer patrolling a private residential area at night. Dispatch notifies you that there is a silent intrusion alarm at a home nearby. The dispatcher says that the resident of the home is on vacation and is not expected to return for at least another week. You respond and leave your patrol car to investigate the outside of the residence. You notice that no lights are on in the house. As you walk around the house checking doors and windows, you come to the back door, which you find to be unlocked, but not forced. (Note to Instructor: Pose this same scenario, but have the officer find the door forced open. Discuss the advisability of entering a possibly burglarized residence and not knowing the status of the threat.) You can see no activity within the house, but you decide to go inside to see if the house has been burglarized.

Using your flashlight, you go from room to room. As you move down the hallway toward the sleeping quarters, a man steps into the hall from one of the bedrooms. He is holding something in his hand, which appears to you to be a gun.

What is your response?

Why?

Is there a better course of action?

What are your alternatives?

Section 7
Decision Making Responsibilities

Learning Goal
The student will understand how common sense, mental preparation and sound tactics can improve an officer's ability to survive and prevail in a deadly force encounter. The student will also understand how proper tactics can reduce the need to use deadly force in certain situations.

The armed private security professional must understand and be able to apply simple tactics that are based on common sense, and have proven effective in armed confrontations. The armed officer must also learn and practice awareness of what is or could be happening in his or her environment. This mental preparation and a working knowledge of tactics is an equally important partner with safe gun handling, competent marksmanship and a thorough understanding of when deadly physical force is justified and necessary. Good tactics may often help the armed officer resolve a potentially deadly situation without resorting to gunfire. In those instances, when shooting is unavoidable, sound tactics can save lives.

Mental Conditioning for Surviving Violent Armed Encounters

Awareness

Many potentially violent situations can be averted by maintaining awareness of who is in your immediate environment, and what is happening around you. If you can maintain the proper degree of alertness and be aware of possible dangers,

you will be able to respond more quickly and effectively. It will help you avoid over-reacting and using unnecessary force. Your ability to see trouble coming has as much effect on the outcome of a violent encounter as any other factor. The problem for most armed private security officers (and law enforcement officers) is remaining alert and aware while fighting boredom. Even in very dangerous locales deadly force encounters are relatively uncommon. The armed officer must maintain situational awareness without appearing suspicious, rude or hyper-vigilant.

Color Code of Awareness: An effective tool for maintaining a useful and sustainable level of mental readiness is the concept. The Color Code was originally developed by members of the 82nd Airborne Division in World War II, and was subsequently adapted to personal defense by Jeff Cooper in the 1960's. The code is characterized by four levels or "conditions" of awareness and readiness.

Each condition is denoted by a color

The first level is **CONDITION WHITE**. In Condition White you are not actively aware of what is happening in your surroundings. You are absorbed in your own private thoughts without giving meaningful attention to the persons around you and what they are doing. Most persons are in Condition White when they are sleeping or in what they consider a secure and safe environment, like the home. Condition White is a potentially disastrous mindset for the on-duty armed officer. While many people go about their daily lives in Condition White, the armed officer cannot afford to disengage from the realities of his or her work environment. In Condition White the armed officer experiences a time lag while he or she becomes aware of the threat, decides that it actually is a threat, and begins to react. This time lag is deadly. The threat will have the initiative, and the officer's reaction will be far behind, maybe too far to act in time to save his or her life. The armed security officer needs an on-duty mental condition that provides tactical awareness and is easily maintained for during the work shift.

While on-duty you should be in **CONDITION YELLOW**, the proper readiness condition for the armed officer. In Condition Yellow you are mentally relaxed, but aware of your surroundings and alert to anything that is unusual or suspicious. In Condition Yellow you realize that you may have to use deadly force to save your life, but you do not know when, how or even if that threat may materialize. Your demeanor is friendly and professional, but you are observing the people in your environment, noticing their actions, and picking up on subtle behavioral clues that might suggest something is not right. Condition Yellow is exactly the mental state in which an armed private security officer should operate. The officer is aware and ready, but calm and in control.

When the armed officer notices that someone or something may be a potential danger, the next level of mental readiness is **CONDITION ORANGE**. In Condition Orange you seek information, investigate and determine whether an actual danger exists. You are ready to use force, deadly force if necessary, and you have a specific potential threat. It is fairly easy to move from Condition Yellow to Condition Orange, but it is difficult to shift from Condition White to Condition Orange. As an example, you are on duty in a shopping mall in August. You are in Condition Yellow: relaxed, but aware. You notice a man in a heavy overcoat. You observe that he stops intermittently and touches his side. You transition into Condition Orange because the heavy coat is unusual for the hot weather, and in your training and experience frequent touching of a garment often indicates that the person is carrying a concealed weapon. In Condition White you are merely at the mall, thinking about the weekend. Even if you do notice the individual in the

coat, you are not thinking about what it might mean. If trouble does erupt, you will not be prepared. Your response will be slow and unsure.

CONDITION RED means that you are justified and ready to shoot if necessary. You have determined that the person may be a deadly threat. You are seeking and using alternatives to deadly physical force, but you are prepared to fire if there is no other safe and reasonable course of action.

If the situation de-escalates and the person leaves without incident, you can then move back to Condition Yellow: relaxed watchfulness.

Stay Focused on the Mission

Anytime anyone, private security officer, law enforcement officer or private citizen, confronts a possibly dangerous situation, there is an element of apprehension. This apprehension is natural and can be a good and useful tool for the armed officer. It is nature's way of preparing you to deal with a threatening situation. It can help you react faster and more decisively. Experiencing apprehension or even fear should not mean freezing in place and being unable to effectively respond. Apprehension is best controlled and utilized by keeping the objectives of your security mission clearly in view.

Remember what you are trying to accomplish. An open or forced door does not require a room to room search, nor does an armed threat mandate a gunfight. The armed private security officer protects by observing, reporting and coordinating assistance. Focus on getting this basic job accomplished. If you think an armed confrontation is imminent or necessary, then try to get help doing it. Manage doubts and fears by performing your duties properly. If, in the course of performing those duties, you must fight for your life or someone else's, then do it. You should realize that dealing directly with the dangerous or deadly threat is not your primary job. It is just something that might happen while you are carrying out your primary responsibilities: observing, reporting, and coordinating.

Be Decisive

Remember that decision you made before assuming the responsibilities of an armed officer that you would be morally and ethically prepared to use your firearm

to protect yourself or another person from a deadly assault? If the time comes that

you must protect yourself (or another person) from an imminent and deadly attack and have no other alternative, then act immediately and fight to win. The only moral and ethical reason for using deadly force is to STOP the threat from killing you or another person NOW. This cannot be done half way. Hesitation in the face

of a deadly attack can be fatal. If deadly force is necessary, use it with the intent to stop the threat IMMEDIATELY.

Basic Tactical Principles

The common sense approach to tactics is embodied in a relative few basic principles. Every armed private security officer must know and practice these proven concepts.

Understand, Recognize and Use Cover and Concealment

Use of cover is a basic tactical principle and is critical to surviving gunfire assaults. ***Cover can be defined as any object that will stop a bullet.*** While your gunfire may stop or divert the threat from his attack, only cover has the ability to stop his bullets from hitting you. Placing an object of cover between you and incoming bullets is always a good idea.

Understanding effective cover is critical. What is cover from one type of firearm may not protect against fire from other, more powerful arms. A stack of wood or a masonry wall may provide protection from handgun bullets, rim-fire rifles and most small shot fired from a shotgun, but it will not reliably stop high-power rifle fire. High powered rifle calibers will penetrate objects that normally stop handgun bullets. While tree trunks, telephone poles, and certain parts of automobiles (engine block, metal wheels or axles) may offer effective cover against handgun bullets, such objects are not total proof against rifle fire. Thick trees, street curbs, heavy steel (like mailboxes and fire hydrants) and concrete are better, but not perfect cover against rifles. ***Both the exterior and interior walls of most residential construction will usually not stop handgun bullets.***

Vehicles appear to offer substantial cover, but passenger cars and light trucks are mostly air inside. The poor cover provided by automobiles is well illustrated by the damage inflicted on police cars and police officers in the 1997 North Hollywood bank robbery shoot-out.

Concealment is any object that can hide you, but is not capable of stopping bullets. Brush, shrubs, sheetrock walls, wooden office or residential doors, and vehicle doors are examples of concealment.

Concealment cannot protect you from incoming fire, but if the threat cannot see you, then he or she may not be able to hit you with gunfire. Also, observation from concealment may allow the officer to control a situation and avoid using deadly force.

The main concern for the armed officer is to not confuse concealment with cover. Humans tend to erroneously believe that if they are hidden, they are protected. If we cannot be seen, we cannot be harmed. To some extent this is true. If a threat cannot see you, then his gunfire will be less accurate or he may decide not to shoot at all. However, the armed officer should not depend on concealment to approach the same protection as even poor cover. For instance, taking cover behind a hollow core door could be fatal.

Soft body armor provides a kind of portable cover, but the armed officer should not depend on it as a sole source of protection. The primary role of soft body armor is to increase the officer's survivability when the assault is immediate and sudden, and there is no opportunity to take cover. If the armed officer has some warning or awareness of a pending attack, then he or she should move to cover. Soft body armor then augments conventional, stationary cover.

It is important that the armed officer practice recognizing cover and using it to best advantage. It is a good idea to locate objects on or near your post or patrol route that would provide useable cover.

In most situations the armed officer should seek cover that retains the officer's ability to keep the threat in view. The ability to see the threat from a cover position allows you to know what the threat is doing and respond appropriately. Losing sight of the threat is dangerous. If you cannot see the threat, he or she may move to a position that would expose you to gunfire, or attack your position directly.

The armed officer must shoot from cover in a position that keeps as much of the officer's body behind the cover as possible. You should practice shooting positions from cover that minimize exposure to incoming gunfire. It is easier to see the threat and minimize exposure by staying several feet behind the cover. A shooting position that is in close contact with the cover ("hugging") requires that you expose more of your body to see and shoot, and it makes movement and manipulation of the handgun more difficult.

corner can conceal a threat. There are two basic techniques for determining if there is an unseen threat around a corner. "Slicing the pie" visualizes a danger point like a corner as the center of a circle. The shooter stands back from the corner and slowly edges into the unseen area by "slicing" off a small arc of the circle at a time. If the shooter believes that a deadly threat exists in the unseen area, then the handgun is in a ready position.

Another useful technique is called the "quick peek". The quick peek is simply a fast look around a corner to see if a threat is present. Sensibly, only the eye on the leading side should be exposed, and the officer should stay back from the corner itself. Once a threat is seen, the officer should maintain cover, keeping the threat in view and ready to shoot if necessary.

Stairways can conceal a threat and are difficult to safely move up and down. If it is necessary to move up or down a stairway, treat it like you would a "horizontal" corner. Slowly approach danger points (landings, overhangs) in short movements, clearing the unseen area a little at a time.

Movement

You reduce the threat's ability to hit you by moving. While most range training is conducted from static, standing positions, dry practice can be devoted to movement away from and to the side of the threat as the handgun is drawn and presented on target. This movement is called "moving off the line of force". The line of force is the threat's natural commitment to attacking you, a stationary target, straight ahead. Moving off this straight-ahead line of attack causes the threat to react and adjust to your actions. This reaction takes time, and you can use that time to bring your weapon into action and get behind cover. Do not make yourself an easy target.

Maximize Distance from the Threat

You gain a tactical advantage by keeping distance between you and the threat. Stay as far back from the threat and potential danger points as possible. You may have to move or retreat to gain that distance. For example, if you have located a deranged person with a knife and are calling for assistance, maintain distance so you can react to a possible attack. Reporting a break-in does not require that you stand right by the point of entry. Standing off a sensible distance will give you some warning of danger. Most criminals are not trained marksmen. Distance makes it harder for them to shoot and hit you.

Barriers

A barrier is, in tactical terms, any object that creates an obstacle to the threat's movement. A barrier prevents or delays an assailant from making contact with you. In this sense, barriers are a kind of cover that stops or delays people, but not bullets. This is especially important when the threat is not openly armed, or is armed with an edged or impact weapon and must close with you to inflict injury. Threats, who appear unarmed, will often attempt to get close to an officer before initiating an assault. Always try place yourself so that some barrier is between you and the possible threat or where the threat could appear. Examples of barriers are furniture, a packing crate, a large planter, a fence or a vehicle. Some barriers can serve as cover if they will stop incoming bullets.

Use Your Senses

You cannot effectively deal with a potentially deadly attack if you are not aware of the threat in time to respond. While your eyes collect much of the information you need about your surroundings, other senses, especially hearing and smell can detect a threat. The actions of the threat that give away his or her presence are called **target indicators**. A hidden threat may give target indicators by inadvertently displaying a piece of clothing, a body part, a part of a weapon or may make a slight noise while moving. You may see the reflection off a pistol or smell alcohol or cigarette smoke. This early detection may give you the time to take cover or retreat.

Avoid Being a Target

If the threat cannot see or find you, it will reduce the opportunity to attack you. Avoid standing out in the open. Minimize or avoid using your flashlight. Often armed officers will mistakenly stand in a lighted space, when it would be safer to seek concealment in a shadowed or darkened area. Avoid movement that rubs your clothing or equipment against a wall. The scraping noise is easily heard and identified. When you check an open door, avoid standing in the doorway. The doorway may be your only option for entering or observing into the room, but standing there and looking around makes you an easy target for a hidden threat. This problem is known as the "fatal funnel" effect. If you must enter a room, get out of the funnel quickly. If you need to look into a room, stand off to the side of the doorway.

Communicate and Obtain Assistance

Several decades ago law enforcement trainers identified a common, but dangerous pattern among some veteran police officers. They called it the "John Wayne Syndrome". This terminology referred to the famous actor's Western movie roles in which he always overcame the bad guy (or bad guys) alone and without any help. After years of single-handedly dealing with tough criminals and always prevailing, many officers developed a sense of invulnerability, which contributed to many officer deaths. The armed private security officer should take heed from these hard learned lessons and seek assistance in handling possibly dangerous persons and situations. It is also vital to communicate with assisting officers, both private security and the police, and provide them with clear and understandable information.

Safe Retreat

If a retreat can be accomplished in relative safety, it can be an effective way to remove the threat's OPPORTUNITY to cause harm. If you believe an armed confrontation is imminent, and only property is at risk, retreat, if safe and practical, can be an effective alternative to force. Retreat can create time and distance for the armed officer to summon assistance. Retreat may also be the necessary and wisest alternative when the threat holds a clear advantage in strength or numbers. On the other hand, there must be a safe place to retreat to.

Retreat can present ethical and moral questions. If your retreat would contribute to the loss of another person's life, then you must decide if that is a morally acceptable option.

Specific Tactical Issues

Ready Positions

In defensive situations you may need to have the handgun out of the holster, in your hand, and ready to use. These uses may include covering the threat at gunpoint, moving with the gun in hand, or being ready to deal with an imminent attack. When the handgun is in your hand and you are under adrenalized, it is imperative that you control the direction the gun is pointing at all times. Using a proper Ready Position will help you control muzzle direction at such times.

Ready Position Safety Concerns

In any ready position you will keep the muzzle pointed in safe direction. Despite the unsafe gun handling seen in Hollywood movies and television police dramas, it is never acceptable to let the weapon point at any non-threat. In a defensive situation this means that you will not allow the muzzle to point at any person unless you have decided that it is necessary to shoot to defend your life or the life of another.

Trigger finger discipline is extremely important in assuming a proper ready position. If you do not intend to fire, the trigger finger must be straight, angled up, and well out of the trigger guard. It is not acceptable to be in a ready position with your finger in the trigger guard.

An unsafe and inefficient position often portrayed in the cinema is the "muzzle up" carry. In this position the muzzle is held up and next to the shooter's head. This mode of carry is not endorsed by any current law enforcement training because of its many liabilities:

1. There is considerable risk of shooting yourself in the head.

2. It is difficult to precisely control the direction of the muzzle.

3. If you stumble or fall, it is difficult to control muzzle direction, and more likely that the gun may discharge in an unsafe direction.

4. It is slower to bring a gun down on target than it is to bring it up to your line of sight. In bringing the gun down gravity pulls the sights past the point of aim, adding movement and wasting time.

5. If the threat attempts to take the gun away from you, your ability to retain control of the gun is hampered by the muzzle up position.

Low Ready Position

The low ready position overcomes most of the problems noted above. The muzzle is pointed down at the ground at an approximately 45-degree angle away from your body. Pointing the handgun in this downward direction minimizes the danger of negligent discharges, and provides an unobstructed view of the threat. Should you need to fire, it is fast and simple to bring the gun up on target. Always remember, however, that even Low Ready can be unsafe if you allow the muzzle to cover another person. For example, you are following another officer as you descend stairs. In that case you should angle the muzzle down and to the side away from the other officer.

SUL Position

SUL is a type of low ready that is useful, but requires proper instruction and practice to employ safely. SUL position has all the advantages of the traditional Low Ready position, and is arguably better adapted to controlling muzzle direction in very close quarters or crowded conditions. The salient safety point in SUL is to keep the wrist bent and the muzzle depressed downward at all times.

Close Ready

Close Ready is useful when you holding an armed and dangerous threat at gunpoint for several minutes while awaiting the arrival of law enforcement. If your arms become too tired to hold the gun up, you can bring the gun into Close Ready to relieve the fatigue. In close quarter encounters Close Ready also allows you to maximize the distance between your handgun and the threat.

Warning Shots

Generally, warning shots are ineffective, potentially dangerous, and are not recommended. A warning shot is especially dangerous if fired into the air. Do you know for certain where it will fall? If you are in immediate danger of death or serious physical injury, time is precious and any shots you fire must be directed at stopping the threat. Warning shots do not usually stop an attacker intent on killing you, and firing a warning shot for anything less than a deadly attack may be unlawful (Recklessly Endangering). Because warning shots are not fired at a person or in a definitely safe direction, they are almost always in violation of the Four Cardinal Safety Rules, especially "Be Sure of Your Target, Back Stop and Beyond."

Shooting at Vehicles

Shooting at a vehicle is not usually effective in stopping the threat. There may be situations in which a moving vehicle is used as weapon against you. Usually the best tactic is to move quickly out of the vehicle's path and take cover behind a substantial barrier. It is difficult to stop a moving vehicle with any small arms fire, and even more so with a handgun. A moving vehicle will continue moving for considerable distances even with its engine and tires shot out. You may be justified in shooting the **driver** of a moving vehicle who is using it to assault you. Also, you may be justified in firing on someone who is firing at you from a moving vehicle. Remember that if you disable or kill the driver, the vehicle will likely continue moving, out of control and possibly causing the death or injury of others. Your decision to shoot must be based on your immediate need to defend yourself or another person, and this decision should be your best alternative available.

Center of Mass

The usual advice given to armed officers is to shoot for the "center of mass". In this sense center of mass means the largest area of the threat's body visible to the shooter. Shooting for the center of mass gives the armed officer the fastest and most accessible point of aim and allows the greatest accuracy error while under the stress of combat. It minimizes the chance of missing and reduces the possibility of hitting an innocent person. In center of mass shooting there is no definitive aiming point like a ten-ring or bullseye. The shooter must quickly determine threat's largest visible body area and fire. The center of mass for an adult human fully facing you would roughly be an imaginary six-inch-wide "pipe" in the center of the torso running between the nipples and the navel. Center of mass shooting is best practiced on the range using realistic, humanoid-type targets without visible scoring rings.

The dynamics of a gunfight do not always provide a classic, fully facing threat. If the threat turns suddenly or is using cover, the largest visible area may be greatly reduced in comparison to the typical police-type target. In this case the officer shoots for the ACM. While the distance between the officer and the threat may be very short, the reduced ACM will require a higher degree of marksmanship and precision. Always use the sights to maximize accuracy.

Standard Response

In a life or death confrontation the armed officer should fire rounds to the center of mass until the threat stops the actions that place the officer or another person in danger of death or serious injury. In practical terms this means that the threat ceases his or her attack on the officer. At that point the armed officer should take cover and issue commands to control the threat. The officer should stay behind cover and not approach a downed assailant until it is determined that he or she is no longer capable of causing harm. If the threat, even if wounded, resumes his or her deadly attack, then the officer is justified in shooting if no other alternative is available.

Multiple Assailants

Law enforcement and armed private security officers are more frequently finding themselves confronted by multiple armed assailants. The primary weapon against multiple threats is officer awareness. The officer is often killed by an undetected second or "back-up" threat. It is also important to understand the guidelines for engaging multiple threats with gunfire. While every situation will be different, the general guideline is to engage the closest threat (if unarmed or armed with a knife or impact weapon) or the more heavily armed threat first. This general rule is subject to change based on the relative danger posed by each threat's weapon and proximity (e.g. a knife at three feet versus handgun at 50 feet).

Body Armor

One of the armed officer's greatest assets is the faithful use of soft body armor. Soft body armor gives the officer the chance to survive the initial gunfire, react, move and effectively retreat or return fire. There are two caveats to the tactical benefit of body armor. First, it must be worn every shift in every season. Body armor left home because it is hot and uncomfortable cannot save lives. Second, the officer must mentally prepare to react and take action if he or she is fired on and hit. While body armor may save an officer from the initial attack, failure to react immediately can result in injury or death.

Use a Safe Holster

At a minimum a proper holster for the armed private security officer should be constructed of quality leather or synthetic materials and be specifically fitted to the make, model and barrel length of the officer's weapon. The holster should have a loop or other attaching device that affixes it tightly and securely to the gun belt. Avoid older model holsters that expose the trigger. These holsters invite a negligent discharge during the draw. The holster should cover the trigger guard, and possess a retaining strap, thumb-break or other positive retention feature. The holster for uniformed duty should be carried on the officer's strong side with the barrel in line with the trouser seam. This carry mode provides quicker access to the gun during the draw, assists a smooth, continuous presentation (draw), and is easier to defend against a take-away attempt. **It is important to remember that there are no "good, cheap" holsters.** Be sure to check your company's policy concerning acceptable duty holsters.

Retention Holsters

A true advancement in officer safety is the modern retention holster. FBI studies suggest that 20-40 percent of police officers are killed with their own handguns. This frightening statistic has fallen in recent years because of the advent of retention holsters and weapon retention training. The retention holster can assist the armed officer in resisting the efforts of a threat to take the gun out of the holster and use it against the officer. As with soft body armor, the armed officer should train in retention techniques. Simply carrying the handgun in a retention holster will not guarantee against a gun take-away.

Moving Threats

A threat that moves and fires at the same time is usually not very accurate. Frequently, the best tactic will be to take cover. However, the armed officer may encounter a situation in which the threat is moving and simultaneously firing at the officer or other persons, and the officer must engage the threat to save lives. Within 30-40 feet the officer should aim for the center of mass, moving the sights with the threat. It is imperative that the officer be absolutely sure of the target, the back stop and beyond. It is never acceptable to endanger innocent persons regardless of the threat's actions.

Moving Under Fire

If you are under fire and you must move (to cover, for instance), look at the point you are moving to, note any obstacles in your path, and then move out as quickly as you can until you reach that location. Running in an erratic pattern will make it more difficult for the threat to hit you. Generally, do not attempt to fire while you are moving. Accuracy will be very poor and you might endanger other persons. Shooting on the move effectively is a skill that requires instruction, coaching and a lot of practice. The armed private security officer is usually best served by moving to cover without delay, and then firing, if necessary, from a stable position.

Safely Retreating with Gun in Hand

If you encounter a deadly or potentially deadly threat, you may decide to retreat with the gun in hand, ready to respond to an attack. Assume a low ready position with the trigger finger outside the trigger guard and alongside the frame. Look quickly to your rear and locate any obstacles or other threats. Look at the threat (or the threat's likely location). Take a large sliding step back with the gun side foot followed by a small step with the support side foot. Repeat this movement until you reach cover or move out of danger. Take very quick (less than one second) looks over your shoulder as you move, but keep your focus on the threat.

Scanning (After-Action Response)

After shooting, stopping and making certain that the assailant is out of action, you should look quickly to each side, and, if possible, behind you to check for other attackers (multiple assailants). This scanning action will help you overcome "tunnel vision", which is the natural inclination to focus your attention on the threat and not recognize what is happening in your peripheral vision.

Section 7: Review

1. Explain how the color code of awareness helps the private security officer mentally prepare to survive a deadly force incident.

2. What is the definition of "cover"? How are cover and concealment different? Why should the private security understand this difference?

3. What are common items that might provide cover against gunfire? How resistant is a residential dwelling (house) to handgun bullets?

4. How does maximizing the distance from the threat work to the officer's advantage?

5. Warning shots are not recommended. Why?

Section 8
Nomenclature & Inspection

Learning Goal
The student will know the components and understand the operation of the service revolver and semi-automatic pistol. The student will understand the importance of inspecting his or her handgun to ensure that it is operational and ready for duty.

Basic Components of the Revolver

The service revolver is comprised of the following main components:

Frame

Includes the trigger and trigger guard, the rear sight, the hammer, firing pin, cylinder latch, and other action parts.

Barrel

Includes the front sight, the rifled bore comprised of lands and grooves, and the muzzle.

Cylinder

Includes the extractor, extractor rod and yoke/crane.

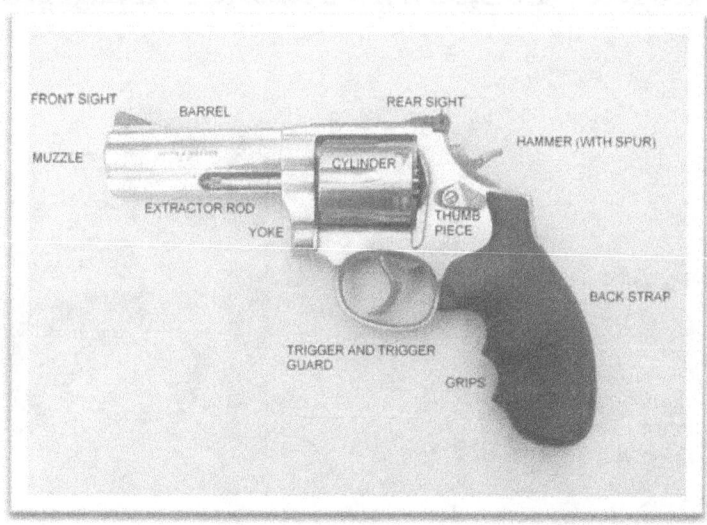

Double-Action Firing Versus Single-Action Firing

The service revolver may be fired in two modes:

Double-Action

The shooter moves the trigger directly to the rear through a relatively long and heavy pull. This long and heavy movement of the trigger partly revolves the cylinder and aligns a cartridge with the rear of the barrel. Simultaneously, the hammer is cycled to the rear of its arc and released, firing the cartridge.

Single-Action

The shooter cocks the hammer (moves it to the rear against spring pressure until it catches the hammer notch), and then exerts a light pressure on the trigger to fire the revolver.

The armed officer may encounter a loaded and cocked revolver and may have to unload it. This situation requires heightened safety consciousness due to the very light single-action trigger pull. The officer should identify a safe direction and back stop to point the revolver during the de-cocking and unloading. This can be a structural part of the building, the ground or a heavy object like a bookcase. All persons should be moved from the area.

TO DE-COCK THE REVOLVER

Pick the revolver up with the trigger finger well away from the trigger guard, and point it in the pre-selected safe direction. Place the support hand thumb between the frame and the cocked hammer, pull the hammer fully to rear, and hold it there while pressing the trigger. Keeping the trigger to the rear, lower the hammer partially and then take the finger off the trigger. Then lower the hammer all the way down. The cylinder can then be opened and unloaded (Removing the finger from the trigger re-engages the internal safeties. If the hammer slips while the trigger is held to the rear, the internal safeties are disengaged and the revolver could fire.)

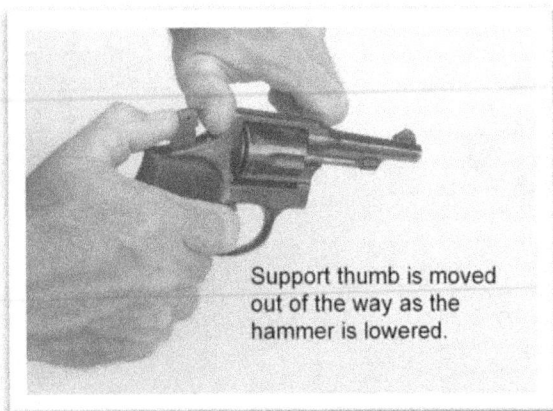

Revolver Inspection:

Before Inspecting The Revolver

1. Point the revolver in a safe direction.
2. Unload and visually and manually check to ensure its unloaded.
3. Remove all live ammunition to a different location before inspecting.

Revolver Serviceability Check

(Bold type indicates corrective action. Armorer repair indicates repair should be performed by a qualified armorer or gunsmith. Factory repair indicates that the repair should be performed by the manufacturer.)

1. Check the overall condition and for visible damage, rust or dirt. **(Clean. Armorer repair.)**

2. Check the stocks for looseness or damage. (Tighten stock screw or replace damaged stocks.)

3. Check the exterior of the barrel for bulges by running the thumb and index finger along the barrel from rear to front. The rear shoulder of the barrel is not a bulge. Check the muzzle for nicks or other damage to the bore. **(Factory repair required.)**

4. Inspect the interior of the barrel (bore) for obstruction. (Remove obstructions like cleaning patches or fouling. Difficult obstructions may require armorer or factory repair.)

5. Inspect the front and rear sights for looseness or damage. **(Armorer repair.)**

6. Inspect the hammer nose (firing pin) for damage or breakage. **(Armorer repair.)**

7. Inspect the recoil plate (firing pin hole) for fouling or damage. **(Clean. Armorer repair.)**

8. Check that the extractor rod moves in and out smoothly without binding. **(Armorer repair.)**

9. The extractor rod may unscrew on Smith and Wesson revolvers. Check for tightness. **(Armorer repair if loose.)**

10. Check the cylinder and its chambers for fouling or damage. The front of the cylinder should be free of fouling. The undersurface of the extractor and its recess in the rear of the cylinder must be free of any fouling, small particles or oil. **(Clean.)**

11. Check that the cylinder opens and closes smoothly without any binding. **(Armorer repair.)**

12. Check all screws for tightness. Be sure to use properly fitted screwdrivers.

13. Check the action for smooth function by dry firing in double-action mode. The trigger should move smoothly to the rear and forward without hesitation or excessive pull weight. The cylinder should carry up to the next chamber and lock in place. **(Armorer repair.)**

Basic Components of the Semi-Automatic Pistol

The semi-automatic pistol is comprised of the following main components:

Frame

Includes the trigger guard, trigger, safeties, de-cocker (SIG-type), hammer, grips, magazine well, magazine catch (release), ejector and slide stop.

Slide

Includes the front and rear sights, recoil spring and guide, extractor, firing pin and decocker (Beretta-type).

Barrel

Includes the chamber, locking lugs, bore and rifling.

Magazine

Includes the magazine body (tube), feed lips, base plate, follower and magazine spring.

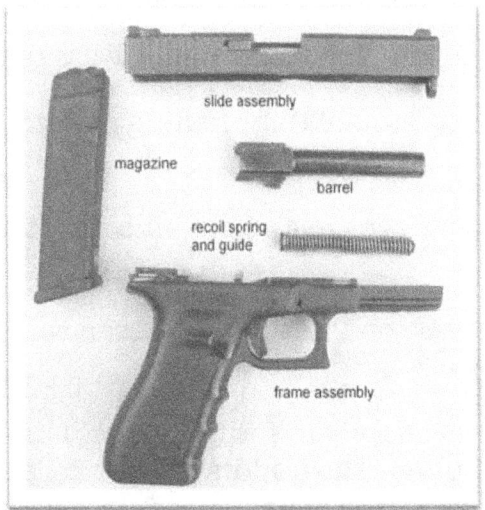

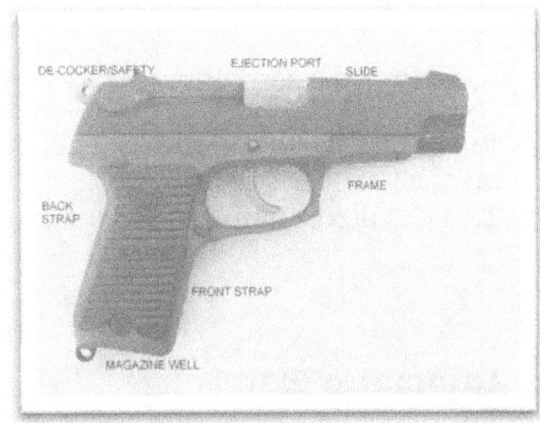

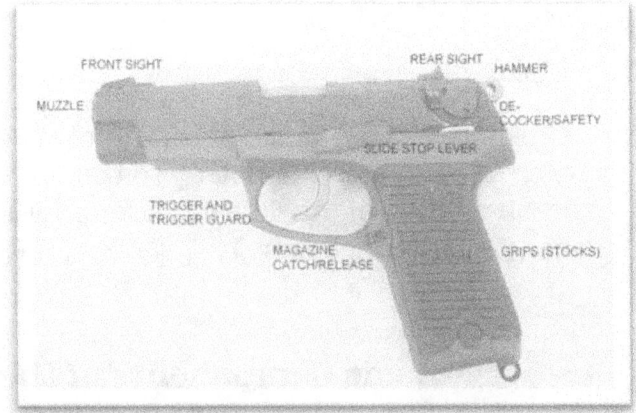

Semi-Automatic Pistol Action Types

Single-Action

Pistol must be manually cocked before firing, and is carried hammer cocked over a loaded chamber with thumb safety engaged.

Double-Action

Pistol is carried with the hammer down on a loaded chamber. Pistol is fired by a long, heavy pull of the trigger for the first round, and then a short, light pull for each subsequent round.

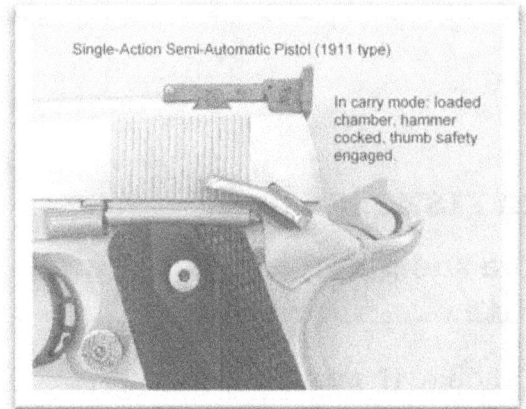
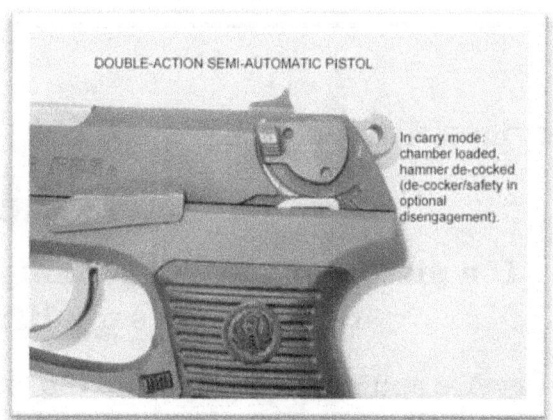

Double-Action Only

Pistol is carried hammer down on a loaded chamber. Pistol is fired by a long, heavy pull of the trigger for each round.

Striker Fired (Glock-type)

Trigger pull retracts the striker against spring compression and then releases the striker for each round fired.

Semi-Automatic Pistol Inspection:

Before Inspecting The Semi-Automatic Pistol
1. Point the revolver in a safe direction. 2. Unload the pistol (removing the magazine, retracting the slide to unload the chamber, lock the slide to the rear, visually and manually check to ensure the magazine well and chamber are unloaded.) 3. Unload all ammunition from the magazine 4. Remove all live ammunition to a different location before inspecting.

Serviceability Checks

ALL SEMI-AUTOMATIC PISTOLS

(If a pistol fails an inspection point, have the pistol inspected and repaired by a qualified gunsmith or armorer.)

1. Dry fire and hold the trigger to the rear. Pull the slide to the rear and allow it to almost close. Release the slide. It should go into battery.
2. Slide forward and hammer down. Insert unloaded magazine. Aggressively pull the slide to the rear and release. Slide should lock open.
3. Press the magazine catch and hold it in. Steel magazines should drop free. Polymer magazines may partially eject.
4. Check the extractor for damage.
5. Check the sights for looseness or damage.
6. Check the slide for small cracks near the ejection port.
7. Check the slide for smooth back and forth movement on the frame rails without binding.
8. Check the exterior of the barrel for bulges, cracks and damage at the muzzle.
9. Check the interior of the barrel for obstructions, fouling and scratches.
10. Check the stocks (grips) for looseness, cracks, chips or missing screws.
11. Check each magazine:
    - Dents, cracks at the top of the back plate and deformed feed lips.
    - Base plate is properly engaged and secure on magazine body.

- Magazine locks up properly in magazine well. Magazines fall free, or are removed with minimal effort (Glock).

12. Check the frame:
    - Ensure that the ejector is in place and not damaged.
    - Cracks near the slide stop hole or notch.
    - Damage to the trigger guard and the magazine well opening.

SPECIFIC SEMI-AUTOMATIC PISTOLS

(If a pistol fails an inspection point, have the pistol inspected and repaired by a qualified gunsmith or armorer.)

Single-action pistols with thumb safety only

(Colt 1911, Browning High Power)

1. Cock the hammer. Engage the safety lever.
2. Pull the trigger. The hammer should not fall.
3. Disengage the safety lever. Pull the trigger. The hammer should fall.

Single-action pistols with a grip safety

(Colt 1911, Springfield XD)

1. Cock the hammer.
2. Pull the trigger without depressing the grip safety.
3. Hammer should not fall.
4. Pull the trigger while depressing the grip safety. The hammer should fall.

Pistols with a slide-mounted decocker/safety lever

(Beretta, S&W)

1. Insert an empty magazine if equipped with a magazine safety (S&W).
2. Cock the hammer. Trigger finger clear of the trigger. Press the decocker/safety lever down. The hammer should fall.
3. Pull the trigger. The hammer should NOT cycle and fall.
4. Push the decocker/safety up. Pull the trigger. The hammer should cycle and fall.

Pistols with a frame-mounted decocker lever

(SIG, H&K)

1. Cock the hammer. Press the decocker down. The hammer should fall.
2. Pull the trigger. The hammer should cycle and fall.

Pistols with a magazine safety

(S&W, Browning)

1. Insert empty magazine. Cock the hammer.
2. Pull the trigger. The hammer should fall.
3. Cock the hammer. Remove the magazine.
4. Pull the trigger. The hammer should not fall.

Pistols with a Glock-type trigger safety

1. Cycle the slide.
2. Move the trigger to the rear without depressing the trigger safety. The striker should not fall.
3. Depress the trigger safety and pull the trigger. The striker should fall.

Modifications to Handguns

The armed private security officer should avoid modifications to the service handgun unless the work is done by the factory or a factory certified gunsmith. If the officer is involved in a shooting, non-factory modifications may create liability for the officer and his or her employer. This liability risk is especially likely when the trigger pull is lightened in an attempt to make the handgun easier to shoot.

The plaintiff's lawyer can claim that the officer acted negligently by carrying a handgun with a "hair trigger" that was more prone to a negligent discharge. It is generally acceptable to enhance the officer's control of the weapon by installing after-market grips that are in general service with law enforcement agencies.

Section 8: Review

1. What are the four steps that must be taken before inspecting any handgun?
2. Why is a light trigger pull a liability risk?
3. Why should the service revolver always be fired in double-action mode?

Section 9
Care & Cleaning

> ### *Learning Goal*
>
> *The student will understand that regular care and cleaning of the duty handgun helps ensure reliable operation in a life threatening situation. The student will be able to identify the proper cleaning procedures for revolvers and semi-automatic pistols.*

Reliability

The primary reason for proper care and cleaning of an armed officer's duty handgun is ensure that it will fire when and if it is needed to protect the officer's life. A handgun is a fairly simple machine, but like any machine, it requires some attention and maintenance for reliable operation. Even modern ammunition produces firing by-products or fouling, which can cause a handgun's mechanism to bind and eventually stop working. The daily carry of a handgun exposes it to heat, cold, moisture, perspiration, dust and other contaminates that can act in concert to prevent the handgun from firing when needed. The professional armed private security officer realizes these facts, and takes personal responsibility for the proper cleaning and lubrication of his or her duty handgun.

General Guidelines for Care and Cleaning

- Handguns should be cleaned after every firing, or, if the handgun is not fired, at least every month. Cleaning may be necessary more frequently depending on climate and working conditions.
- Handguns should be inspected by a qualified, factory trained armorer at least once annually.
- Check with your employer regarding disassembly. Detail stripping should be avoided.

- Clean your handgun in a place where other persons will not interrupt you or gain access to your handgun.

1. **Ensure that your handgun is unloaded before cleaning. Gun Cleaning Safety.** The four Cardinal Safety Rules apply every time you clean your duty handgun. You must safely unload your gun prior to cleaning or disassembly. Note that some semi-automatic pistols (like the Glock) require that the user pull the trigger in order to disassemble the gun. This means that the user must have safe back stop to unload the pistol, point it and pull the trigger before disassembly.

2. **Remove all ammunition from the gun and immediate area.** The gun must be unloaded, the magazines emptied, the duty belt and speed-loaders or magazines removed from sight and reach. Verify that the gun is unloaded by looking and touching. Place your smallest finger in the chamber of a semi-automatic pistol. It is possible for a mechanical defect to allow a cartridge to remain in the chamber.

3. **Permit no distractions during the unloading and cleaning process.** If you are interrupted during the unloading or cleaning, you must go back to go back to the beginning of this ritual to verify again that the gun is unloaded. Interruptions may lead to an accident. These interruptions include taking phone calls, watching television, having visitors or children come in. What often happens is that the gun is loaded at some point just before or during the interruption, and the user does not remember that the gun is loaded when he or she returns to it after the interruption. The user of the gun then treats the gun as if it is unloaded (a violation of a Cardinal Safety Rule!) and negligently fires it.

4. **Make a conscious switch to *Cleaning Mode*.** Tell yourself out loud that the gun is unloaded for the purpose of cleaning.

5. You must have a safe, bullet-stopping aim point if you will dry fire the gun during the disassembly, cleaning and re-assembly process. Soft body armor works well in this role. The gun should only be pointed at something you are willing to destroy.

6. **Once you have cleaned, re-assembled and loaded the gun, make a conscious mental switch.** Say out loud: "The gun is loaded and will fire if I pull the trigger." You must impress on yourself that the gun is loaded and ready to fire. This action will help you remember that the gun is "hot" should you be interrupted. (At least two highly trained federal officers have shot themselves in recent months while handling or cleaning their handguns. In each case the officer assumed that the pistol was unloaded, when the officer had in fact loaded it not long before the incident.)

7. **When the handgun is re-assembled, you should safely store it immediately whether it is loaded or not.** The gun should be holstered or cased, and removed from sight and reach. If you leave it lying around, there will be a subconscious temptation to pick it up and dry fire. You think that you will remember, but many have not.

8. There are no shortcuts to gun safety. If you follow the above ritual every time, you will avoid a negligent discharge and possibly a tragedy.

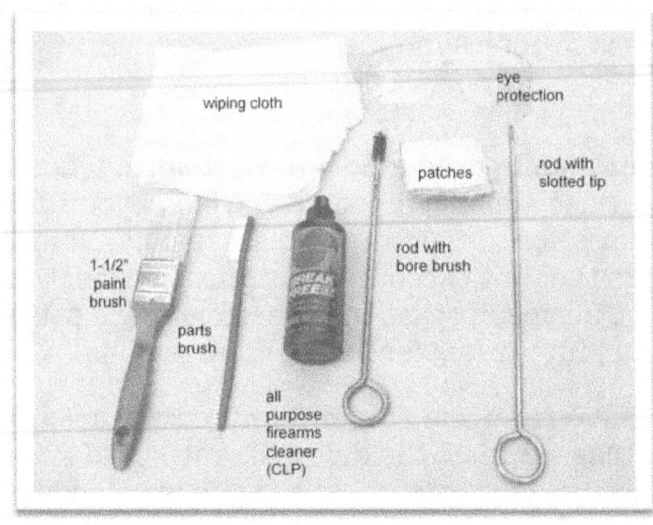

Revolver Cleaning Procedure

Barrel

1. Attach a properly fitted bore brush to the cleaning rod. Place a few drops of bore cleaning solvent on the bore brush (a CLP product like BreakFree ™ is useful as a solvent, lubricant and preservative). Working from the muzzle, push

2. the bore brush completely through the barrel and then completely pull it out. Repeat six to eight times. (Avoid pushing the rod so hard that it slams against the recoil shield.)

3. Attach a slotted tip or patch puller to the cleaning rod and push a dry cotton or flannel patch through the bore several times. It will "mop" up the CLP and fouling, and will come out very dark and dirty. Follow with another dry patch to ensure that the bore is dry and free of CLP.

4. Use a weapons cleaning brush (toothbrush-type) to clean the back of the barrel or forcing cone, under the top strap, the recoil shield, around the firing pin hole and the muzzle. Wipe thoroughly with the dry cloth.

Cylinder

1. Clean each chamber (or charge hole) like the barrel above. Be certain to wipe each chamber dry with a clean patch. Excessive solvent (CLP) left in the chambers can deactivate the primer and powder charge.

2. Brush off the face of the cylinder. Do not use a steel wire brush. Wipe with a dry cloth.

3. Clean under the extractor and its recess in the cylinder. A small, clean paint brush is useful. DO NOT ALLOW ANY CLP TO REMAIN UNDER THE EXTRACTOR. It will attract debris and fouling, which can bind the cylinder to a stop.

Frame

1. The recoil plate or shield should be brushed well. Special attention should be given to the hammer nose, hammer nose bushing hole and bolt pivot hole to ensure that no residue is left in these areas. Wipe with a dry cloth.

2. Brush the rear sight and any recesses on the exterior of the frame.

Yoke

1. Brush the yoke (crane) and wipe with a dry cloth.

2. Apply a small drop of CLP to the extractor rod and work the rod back and forth.

Stocks

1. Remove the stocks and thoroughly brush the frame underneath. Rust and dirt will accumulate.

2. Before re-installing the stocks on Smith and Wesson revolvers, check the strain screw. It must be tight to ensure reliable primer ignition.

Lubrication

1. Revolvers require little lubrication. Over-lubrication attracts dirt and fouling, and can cause the action to become sluggish and produce misfires.

2. Apply a small drop of CLP (tip of toothpick) into the frame in front of the cocked hammer and in front of the trigger (in cocked condition).

3. Wipe all external surfaces with a dry, clean cloth.

Semi-Automatic Cleaning Procedure

Barrel and Chamber

1. Clean with a properly fitting bore brush. Place a few drops of CLP on the bore brush and push it completely through the barrel from rear to front several times. Wipe out the brushed bore with two dry cotton or flannel patches.

2. Use a brush and CLP to clean all powder residue from the barrel ramp, locking lugs, muzzle and adjacent surfaces.

Frame

1. The interior of the frame should be brushed out using a small paint or chip brush. A can of compressed air is useful in removing residue.

2. Brush the slide rails free of residue and fouling.

3. Brush the ejector free of fouling.

4. Wrap the cleaning rod with a clean cloth to clean the interior of the magazine well.

5. Wipe the exterior and accessible interior portions with a clean, dry cloth.

Slide

1. Brush out the grooves that engage the frame rails.

2. Brush the breech face and firing pin (striker) hole. Keep the slide oriented muzzle down so that fouling and debris do not fall into the firing pin hole and then into the firing pin channel. This can cause a sluggish firing pin or striker and subsequent misfires.

3. Brush under the extractor hook. Be careful to remove all fouling and residue particles.

4. Use a small paint brush or chip brush to brush out the interior surfaces of the slide.

5. Lightly brush the front and rear sights using a soft nylon toothbrush.

6. Wipe all interior and exterior surfaces with a clean, dry cloth.

Magazines

1. Magazines can be primary causes of malfunctions. It is helpful to number your magazines to isolate any that may be causing malfunctions. Do not carry a faulty magazine on duty.

2. Magazines should be disassembled and cleaned periodically or when subjected to very wet or sandy conditions. Check with your employer before you do this. Follow the magazine disassembly procedures in your pistol's owner's manual.

3. The exterior and interior surfaces of the magazine should be cleaned and wiped dry. Do not oil the interior of the magazine. The magazine spring may be wiped with a lightly oiled cloth.

Lubrication

1. Semi-automatic pistols require some limited lubrication.

2. One drop of CLP should be applied to the exterior of the barrel and rubbed over all surfaces. Ensure that the locking lugs receive a

3. small drop of lubrication.

4. One small drop of CLP should be applied to each frame rail.

5. One small drop of CLP should be rubbed on the interior bearing surfaces of the slide (these are the surfaces that have the finish worn off).

6. Wipe the entire exterior surface of the pistol with a clean, dry cloth.

Care of Ammunition

General Considerations

1. **Use only factory manufactured ammunition on duty.** Factory manufactured, new ammunition has passed many reliability and safety inspections, and helps defend the armed officer from allegations of excessive or malicious force. Generally, the brands and types of ammunition in use by local law enforcement agencies is a good selection guide. Reloaded ammunition from a reputable supplier may be adequate for practice, but should never be carried as duty ammo.

2. Prior to carrying a new type or brand of ammunition, you should test it in your semi-automatic by firing rounds from all your duty magazines. All rounds from all magazines should fire and operate with 100% reliability.

3. **Duty ammunition should be changed out on an annual basis.** The old duty ammunition, if in good condition, can be fired in practice or qualification.

4. **Your employer may specify a particular brand and/or type of ammunition, and you should follow that direction.** If you substitute your employer's ammunition with your own preferred ammo, you may face personal liability in the event of a shooting.

Inspection of Ammunition

1. **Visually inspect every round of duty ammunition before carrying it on duty.** New manufactured ammunition is generally of very high quality, but defects may escape detection at the factory.

2. Check each round:
   - Check that each round has a **primer properly seated flush** with the base of the cartridge.
   - Check for cracks, dents or splits in the case body.
   - Check for bullets that are **seated more deeply or shallow** than others.

3. A cartridge with any of the above defects should be rejected.

Cleaning Ammunition

1. Ammunition should be wiped off with a dry, clean cloth.

2. Do not oil, wax or apply any coating to ammunition. This could cause failures to fire.

3. Store ammunition in a secure location in the factory container or a container specifically made for ammunition. Temperature extremes and dampness should be avoided.

Section 9: Review

1. What is the primary reason for proper care and cleaning of the service handgun?

2. What steps should be taken to ensure safety before the handgun is cleaned?

3. Why should the private security officer carry only factory manufactured ammunition on duty?

Section 10
Low Light Shooting

Learning Goal
The student will understand that positive identification of a person as an immediate deadly threat is more difficult in low light conditions. The student will understand how the General Flashlight Rules can enhance officer safety and effectiveness in low light conditions. The student will learn that the flashlight's primary purpose is to provide the armed officer with information, and that the secondary purpose of the flashlight is to assist low light shooting accuracy.

The majority of law enforcement and private security operations are conducted during night hours or low light environments like warehouses, attics and basements. Even armed private security officers working daytime shifts will eventually encounter dark conditions, often in an emergency situation. Over 70% of law enforcement shootings occur in low light conditions.

Low Light Environments Present Special Problems for the Armed Officer

It is much more difficult to see if a person is armed and presents an immediate threat. **Especially in low light conditions, you must positively identify the person as an armed threat before using deadly force. Shooting at a person you have not identified is never permissible.**

It is more difficult to fire accurately. Manipulation of the flashlight and handgun during firing and reloading also require training and practice. Like a handgun, mere possession of a flashlight does not mean that an armed officer is competent in its use. Effective flashlight technique requires thought and preparation.

General Flashlight Use Guide

The General Flashlight Guide provides basic guidelines on the effective use of the flashlight in a defensive environment. Like any guidelines, there are exceptions. The armed officer must use sound judgment in applying the following rules and techniques.

Purpose of the Flashlight

Humans can see in dark or low light conditions, but not very well. The primary purpose of the flashlight is to allow the armed officer to see better in dark or low light situations. While a flashlight cannot provide the quality of daylight or even good indoor lighting, it can help the armed officer gather enough information about a person to determine if that person is armed and presents an immediate deadly threat. It is important to understand that the flashlight may or may not enhance an officer's ability to shoot accurately in low light. In some instances, holding a flashlight while shooting may compromise an ideal shooting grip, but the advantages of light outweigh the gun handling issues.

Have a Flashlight

1. Carry a flashlight at all times on duty. If you are working a night shift or a low light environment, the full size duty flashlight should be your primary light. During daytime hours a small belt light will prove useful when working in situations that are dark or have restricted access.

2. Carry an extra flashlight on your person. Any experienced private security or law enforcement officer can tell you that even the most reliable flashlight will fail when you have the most need of it. Law enforcement trainers caution officers that "Two is one, and one is none." Think about it.

Keep the Flashlight in Your Possession

1. Always keep the flashlight on your person and under your control.

2. Avoid laying the flashlight down to do a task. First, place it back in its holder or ring. If the flashlight rolls away or falls, it will be difficult to find in the darkness.

Hold the Flashlight in Your Support (Non-Gun) Hand

Keep your strong hand (gun hand) free in case you have to fire.

Avoid Over Use of the Flashlight

1. Avoid activating the flashlight and leaving it on continuously while you search or carry out other tasks. The continuous light will quickly drain the batteries, and can attract hostile fire.

2. Hold the switch partly down to turn the light on momentarily. Releasing pressure on the switch allows you to turn the flashlight off instantly.

3. "Pulse the switch." Turn the flashlight on for no more than two seconds. Observe, and then turn the flashlight off. Pulsing the switch will allow you to see, and reduce the threat's ability to follow your movements.

Avoid Illuminating Other Officers

1. Take care to direct your flashlight away from other officers. Your light can make them easy targets for the threat, and gives away their position and yours.

2. Use ambient light (indirect light from other sources: street lights, vehicle lights, parking lot lights, moonlight, other officer's flashlights) for general observation. Save your light for specific observation. Be a "light vulture."

After Firing or Using the Flashlight Turn It Off and Move

1. While your flashlight helps you see the threat, it can attract hostile fire from the threat or an accomplice. Once you have seen what you need to see, turn it off.

2. Practice moving immediately after you use the light or fire. Even a step or two can prevent the threat from hitting you if he fires at the last known location of your light.

The Light/Darkness General Guideline

1. This guideline is intended to give the armed officer the basic concept for using the flashlight in typical low light environments. It should not be accepted as a strict rule. A specific situation may dictate a different approach to using the flashlight.

2. Most low light environments have areas of darkness or shadow, and areas of relative light. If you are in a dark area, do not use your light, but use the darkness for concealment. Look into the lighted areas. You can see fairly well without a flashlight, and you will stay concealed from the threat.

3. If you are in a lighted area, you have no concealment in the darkness. You are already easily seen by the threat. Move to cover, and use the flashlight to illuminate the shadowed or darkened areas.

Flashlight Firing Techniques

Flashlight firing techniques can be separated into two categories:

- **Firing with the flashlight and handgun held separately:** These techniques are usually employed when the armed officer is searching or generally observing, and is suddenly confronted by a threat and must fire immediately.

- **Firing with the flashlight and handgun held together:** These techniques are usually employed when the armed officer has located a threat and has time to get into position.

Firing with the Flashlight and Handgun Held Separately

The most commonly used techniques were developed by the FBI several decades ago. These techniques are adaptable to most large and small flashlights, and they are currently still taught by most law enforcement academies.

1. **FBI HIGH:** This technique is useful for searching or general observation in situations where the officer is looking down or into a lower area like high grass or down a staircase. A benefit of this technique is that it positions the light away from the officer's center of mass. It is also adaptable to all types of flashlights including small belt flashlights with end-cap switches.

2. **FBI LOW:** This technique is useful for searching or general observation on level terrain or in situations where the officer is looking upward. It also places the light away from the officer's center of mass. It is best adapted to full size flashlights with the switch on the barrel or head. It can be awkward for some officers to employ this technique with small, belt flashlights with end-cap switches.

FBI High Searching

FBI High On target

FBI Low Searching

FBI Low On Target

Firing with the Flashlight and Handgun Held Together

There are three basic techniques that hold the flashlight and handgun together or in close proximity to each other. The purpose is to approximate the steadiness of a two-handed firing grip and provide improved recoil control. One of the three techniques is specific to small belt flashlights with end-cap switches.

Each of the following techniques works best when teamed with one of the FBI techniques. While the following techniques can be used for general searching and observation, they can be fatiguing. The FBI techniques require less muscular effort, and are best used for searching/observation role. The officer can then transition to the appropriate flashlight/handgun technique when a specific threat is confronted.

1. **HARRIES TECHNIQUE:** This technique can be assumed as the handgun is drawn from the holster, or the officer can transition into it from the FBI HIGH technique. It steadies the officer's firing platform and provides fairly good recoil control. **The HARRIES TECHNIQUE is very useful when the officer must fire around cover from his strong side.**

It is important that the officer extend the handgun on target first and then bring the flashlight wrist under the gun wrist. Placing the flashlight on target first and then extending the handgun will allow the muzzle to cross the officer's gun hand! This is improper and very dangerous.

Assuming the Harries Technique. Gun out, then flashlight moves under.

Harries Technique On target.

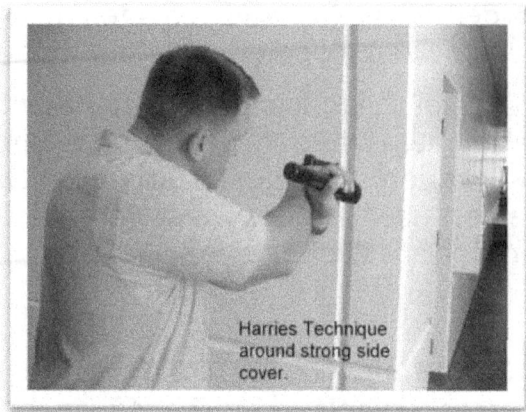

2. **SIDE BY SIDE TECHNIQUE:** This technique can be assumed as the handgun is drawn from the holster, or the officer can transition into it from the FBI LOW

technique. It is quick to assume, and it tends to place the beam high in the threat's eyes. **It is also useful when the officer must fire around cover from the support side.**

Side by Side Technique: note downward angle of support wrist.

Side by Side Technique: firing around support side cover.

3. **BELT FLASHLIGHTS WITH TAIL-CAP SWITCH:** Because of the location of the switch in the tail-cap, these smaller flashlights are best used with the FBI HIGH and HARRIES TECHNIQUE. If the tail-cap switch protrudes enough, the officer can use a technique known as the ROGERS or SYRINGE TECHNIQUE. If the tail-cap switch does not protrude, the officer can use the SIDE BY SIDE VARIATION. **These techniques are also useful when firing around cover from the officer's support side.**

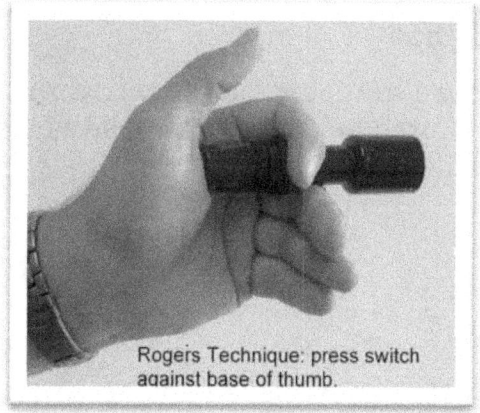
Rogers Technique: press switch against base of thumb.

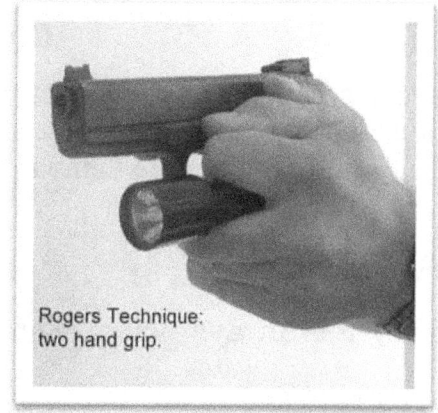
Rogers Technique: two hand grip.

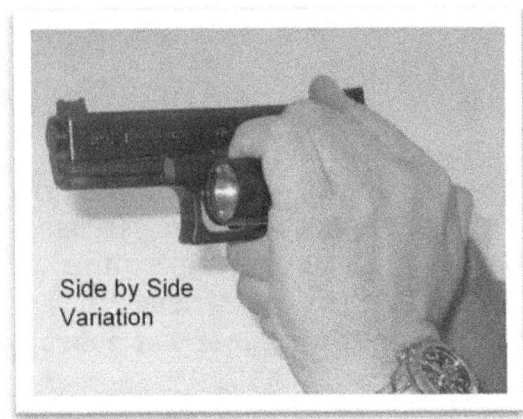

Gun Mounted Lights

There are various light systems that can be attached to the frame (dust cover) of semi-automatic pistols. Like any technology gun mounted lights have both advantages and disadvantages for the armed private security officer.

Advantages

1. The light is always available on the handgun.

2. Normal firing grip and technique can used, which enhances speed and accuracy.

3. One hand controls both the gun and the light, leaving the other hand available for other tasks.

Disadvantages

1. 1. The handgun is automatically pointed at anything or person which is illuminated by the light. Any person illuminated by the gun mounted light will be at gunpoint. If that person is not a verified deadly threat, the officer will have violated the law

(Pointing a Firearm at Another). This factor is a major disadvantage for the private security officer, who may legally point a firearm at another person only if that person is a deadly threat.

2. The gun mounted light is restricted to situations in which the armed officer has identified a person as a deadly threat, and has the justification and necessity to use deadly physical force.

3. The light should be carried mounted on the handgun at all times, which will require a special holster. If the handgun and light are carried separately, the light is mounted as the need is perceived. It must then be dismounted before the handgun can be holstered. If the armed officer must defend him or herself with less lethal force, it will be difficult if not impossible to re-holster the gun in a fighting situation.

Low Light Firing without a Flashlight

A trained armed officer can effectively engage and hit a threat in low light conditions without the aid of a flashlight. The light from streetlights, buildings and vehicles can provide enough light to use the sights and hit. Without the flashlight, however, it is difficult in low light conditions to determine if a person is armed and presents a deadly threat. Firing without the aid of a flashlight will probably be restricted to situations in which the threat is already firing on the officer and there is neither time nor need to employ the flashlight.

The effectiveness of firing in low light conditions without the flashlight can be enhanced making the sights more visible to the shooter and/or employing low light specific techniques:

1. Equipping the handgun with (tritium) night sights.

2. Painting the front sight with white or luminescent paint to make it more visible.

3. Using the instance of muzzle flash to verify alignment of the sights.

4. Aligning the sights against a lighter background, and then moving that image on to the target.

5. Using stance directed fire (unsighted) at close ranges.

Reloading and Clearing Malfunctions

1. Turn the flashlight off and move. If cover is available, use it.

2. If your flashlight is full size, place it high under your strong arm with the lens facing forward. If your flashlight is a small belt light, it can be difficult to retrieve from under your arm. An alternative is to place it in a pocket or in its sheath or holder.

3. After reloading or clearing the malfunction retrieve the flashlight and assume one of the flashlight firing techniques.

Firing around Corners with the Flashlight

It may be necessary for an armed private security officer to fire around the corner of a building or, if the officer is moving or retreating, to observe around the corner and be ready to fire if necessary. It is important that the armed officer expose as little of his or body as possible to the threat. An accepted method of clearing a corner is the "slice the pie" technique. To slice the pie the officer places him or herself in a low ready position at least three or more feet from the corner and then moves in small arcs around the apex of the corner. Each arc or movement exposes an additional slice or area to the officer's view.

It is important that the beam of the flashlight enter the exposed area slightly ahead of the gun. This will prevent the light from "splashing" off the cover and impairing the officer's vision. The Harries Technique works best when clearing a corner on the officer's strong side (right side for a right handed shooter), and the Side By Side Technique works best when clearing a corner on the officer's support side.

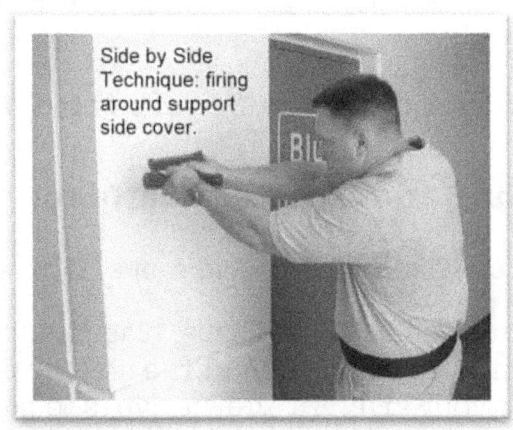

Section 10:   Review

1. Why does a low light environment present special problems when encountering a possible threat?

2. What does "Two is one and one is none" mean?

3. Generally, an officer concealed by dark shadows should not turn the flashlight on. Why?

4. What is the legal issue if a gun-mounted light is improperly used to illuminate non-threat persons?

Section 11
Training For Tomorrow

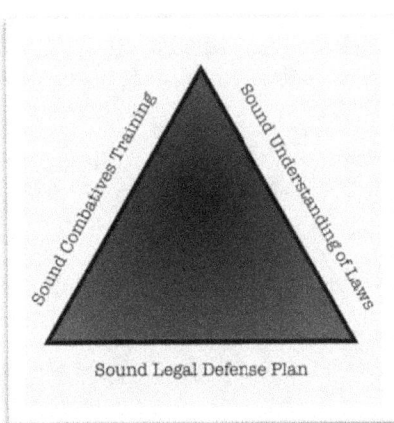

In discussing the topic of Firearms Self-Defense, most people unintentionally focus on only one aspect, the 'Purchase' of a firearm. Unfortunately, the vast majority of armed citizens completely ignore three other equally important elements:

1. Without sound combatives training, your fancy new firearm is useless and in all reality it places you and others at greater risk.

2. Without sound understanding of the laws associated with Self-Defense, there's no way for you to develop a decision making process, which provides reasonable responses to perceived threats.

3. Without a sound Legal Defense plan, should you be forced to actually use Deadly Force in defense of your life or someone else's, your entire Legal Defense strategy will be based on 'Chance'.

The intent of this chapter is to point-out (3) important elements to 'Sound Combatives Training':

1. Firearms Kata
2. Stress Inoculation
3. Tactical Training

Your Self-Defense Response to tomorrow's deadly threat is determined by what you do today, to assure it's the 'Best' response capable of overcoming even the most extreme circumstances tomorrow. Determining what response is 'Best' and what method of training has the greatest potential to condition the 'Right' response, is the most essential decision you'll make.

Today there is a smorgasbord of training systems and methodologies. Sadly, that's how most people approach the concept of 'Firearms Training', as though it were a meal or a means of filling one's appetite. Other's approach it from a most passive perspective of simply learning to shoot accurately or draw quickly and completely overlook the 'Fight' in tomorrow's Fight. You see most people fail to realize just how significate this type of training actually is because they don't take the time to first process and digest exactly 'What' they're training for. When it comes to Firearms Self-Defense, the reality is that said 'Training' is supposed to give you the ability to provide a perfect response to a completely random, surprised attack on your actual existence. The gravity of such an attack is such that your 'Response' is your ONLY hope for survival. So selection of the 'Right' training method boils down to determining how much your 'Life' means to you.

When it relates to Firearms Self-Defense, the word 'Training' is often where people get tripped up. Since its use is so common, embodying all forms of instruction and schooling, from everyday academics to sports and even vocational, the concept of 'Training' is easily misunderstood when it comes to Self-Defense. When it relates to Self-Defense, it's meaning has a depth and density, which simply can't be compared to any other form.

As was just stated, training for tomorrow's battle means your attempting to develop a physical response to a completely unknown future circumstance, that poses an immediate threat to your actual existence. What this means is that you must develop a 'Perfect' response to a completely unknown situation, where 'Second Place' means you lose and loosing means you die.

Other forms of training such as academics, sports or vocational type instruction, all allow for a particular degree of error. For instance, academically the standard is a (C), as long as you maintain that average, you pass. Obviously a (B) or (A) would result in a much more competitive outcome, giving you higher placement amongst your peer-group. However, when it relates to an actual fight for your life, your level of proficiency MUST translate to 'Straight A's' and when the test comes, the ONLY acceptable outcome is an (A+). If you do not meet that standard, the only probable outcome is death. It's really that simple. Are there people who survive battles with no preparation at all? Yes. However, theirs is all based on 'Chance'. Ask yourself this, would you bet your life on a game of Craps, would you wager it all away on one roll of the dice? If your answer was yes, this training's not for you. However, if your answer was like the vast majority of other reasonably minded individuals, then this chapter should be studied and re-studied, so you arrive at the 'Right' decision.

Firearms Kata...

Your first step towards developing a squared away Self-Defense Response, begins with understanding the composition of Firearms Self-Defense as a whole. Once you've fully grasped the realization, that the act of 'Using' a firearm to defend oneself, requires both a Physical and Psychological process, then you're able to go about honing each aspect with intelligence and an acute attention to detail.

Let's dissect the 'Physical' component or the 'Kinesis' of firearms. Of course, what we all hope for is to somehow acquire an instantaneous response or 'Reflex' to an immediate and deadly threat. Much like the 'Patellar Reflex Test' your doctor does when they tap your knee with that rubber mallet, we hope to develop a defense mechanism that fires immediately upon first contact and hits the mark accurately and without error. Now we all know that nobody is born a fighter or an expert shot, all that is acquired through training. So the obvious question is, which training method is best? When it relates to the kinesis of shooting; the culmination of isolated movements for one overall response, there are a plethora of methods available.

Unfortunately, the vast majority of firearms training methods prove to be counterproductive and in many cases actually place the trainee in a much more compromised position than if they wouldn't have even trained at all. It's been said that "Practice Makes Perfect" so many are fooled into believing that if something looks good on paper or the masses support it, then it's got to be worth their time and money. Well, I'd wager that 'Poor Practice' is the fastest way to learn how to lose and in this arena, losing gets you dead. Instead of conditioning appropriate responses, most training methods place the trainee at a disadvantage, where they wind-up wasting time, money and effort, all while conditioning responses, which not only attempt to violate the Laws of Physics, but rely on concepts and movements which are completely impossible to reproduce during an actual real-life fight.

Have you ever wondered how Michael Jordan became the super star he was and still is? During an interview, Jordan claimed that the only way he became so good at his craft, was because his mother made him shoot 'Free Throws' every day as child for hours at a time. This concept; 'Free Throws' and its relationship with Firearms Self-Defense is vitally important to grasp.

A Free Throw costs nothing and is a 'Free' attempt at an easy point. As an added bonus, all 'Time' stops and everyone waits for the shooter to concentrate and take his time for two perfect shots. In the NBA, most games often rely on a team's ability to sink these all important 'Free' shots. In any given game you'll see dozens of attempts, where each individual player employs their own unique style. What's different about the Free Throw is the cadence and sequence by which each shooter shoots. As opposed to any other shot, players tend to shoot their Free Throws the exact same way each and every time, time after time, game after game, through their entire careers. You'll notice they each have their own individual way of doing what they do and they do it the same way each time. For instance, a given player will bend their knees and crouch the same way each time. They will bounce the ball in the same manner and the same amount of times prior to the shot. They'll pause for the same amount of time before extending and releasing, in the same manner each and every time.

What's interesting is the manner by which Jordan grew-up practicing his Free Throws. He took this practice to Zen like state of training. He obviously understood the concept of 'Kata'. He polished and honed his shot, so well that in a 1991 game against the Denver Nuggets, he taunted; then rival Dikembe Mutombo, by saying "Hey, Mutombo. This one's for you" He closed his eyes and sunk the shot like nobody's business and followed it up with his pearly whites as he arrogantly smiled back at Mutombo to win the game.

While there might not be some sort of 'Holy Grail', there is a method which far outweighs any of today's more common approaches. At the very least you should invest your time in learning about this approach, adopt its principles and infuse them into your training regime. Dry-Fire Training is to Shooting what the Free Throw is to basketball. If you had to choose (1) method of learning to 'Shoot' and manipulate a firearm, Dry-Fire Training or 'Snapping In' is your BEST choice.

Dry-Fire Training is how one fine tunes and hones their craft and it's the best way to win the fight ahead of time. Dry-Fire Training derives its name from the fact that the trainee presses the trigger on an empty or 'Dry' chamber, meaning there's a complete absence of ammunition. This affords you the ability to practice Trigger Manipulation without the need for ammunition, thereby completely avoiding the need for a firearms range. Just like with basketball Free Throws, all 'Time' stops. You have all the time in the world today, to isolate and perfect each and every individual element, which makes-up the overall movement or function, for that perfect shot tomorrow. You, determine how long it takes to perform said movements and how focused your attention to detail actually is. Best of all Dry-Fire Training is 'Free', can be done from home and is hands down the best way to master one's Kata.

Now I know what you're thinking, how is it possible to learn how to defend one's self with a gun, by shooting an empty one at home? Don't you need to master 'Recoil' and actually shoot at targets to know what real bullets actually do? The simple answer is, NO! All bullets do the exact same thing every single time. When the round's primer is struck by the firing pin, the primer initiates a series of controlled explosions, thereby propelling the projectile; or bullet, down the barrel. Once the projectile clears the muzzle, gravity and wind is all that matters. Like bullets, the Recoil of a given caliber of ammunition is the exact same every time in your particular firearm. When the round initiates, physics causes the energy of the explosion, to force the firearm up and back towards you at the very same rate and pitch each and every time. How you go about controlling recoil and sending an accurate round downrange has less to do about 'Shooting' and EVERYTHING to do about what you do 'Physically' to the firearm prior to the round ever being fired. Meaning, what matters most is the perfection of 'Kinesis' not making the gun go bang.

What traditional firearms training does, is attempt to teach a person to learn how to do something 'Right' by first doing something 'Wrong'. What I mean is, they take a novice to a firing range, hand them a loaded firearm, give them verbal instruction on how their supposed to 'Physically' manipulate said firearm, then tell them to "FIRE". What do you think happens? They miss. Now the instructor goes about attempting to erase the miss through further verbal instruction and has them fire again and again and again until they 'Miss' more accurately. That's what you call learning to do something wrong, expensively.

Some of the best Snipers in history come from Russia. They have consistently produced the deadliest shooters in the greatest numbers since WWI. The reason has to do with 'How' they condition their Snipers. Instead of giving them a box of ammunition and sending them to the range, they spend the vast majority of their time Dry-Firing. Then when the 'Test' comes, they're given them ONE round because the first round is the only round that matters.

When a person Dry-Fires a weapon over and over and over, their body begins to 'Feel' its way around the enigma of mastery. Dry-Fire is what breaks the code, while their body feels its way into perfect harmony of that particular firearm's mechanics and its relationship to a given person's own body mechanics. Overtime the two become one and they've become the weapon.

The difference between a Dry-Fire shooter and your typical firearms shooter is that the traditional shooter is forever plagued by recoil. Because the traditional shooter has attempted to learn how to master their firearm under the explosive influence of recoil, they're hands and intern the rest of their body has not been able to 'Feel' the relationship between the perfect grip and trigger squeeze as the firearm is in perfect alignment with their wrists, arms, shoulders and eyes. Periodically, the traditional shooter my feel one or two components of harmonious kinesis, however the effects of recoil completely prevent them from feeling all of these vital elements at once. However, the Dry-Fire shooter, simply loads their firearm, and manipulates it as though there were no bullet at all. To them, what they do 'Before' recoil is all that matters. Their bodies have already memorized how to perfectly feel it's way through the sequence of movements for that harmonious shot.

However, traditional Dry-Fire Training systems fall short and do not provide the totality of training required to master the 'Combatives' of Firearms Self-Defense. Similarly, there are a hand-full of other training methods; like the 'Four Point Draw', which delve into the concepts of Kata, but still fail to provide the density required for an actual fight. Likewise, they also fall short and don't offer a total-training-system like Japanese Aikido. Traditional approaches focus on the 'Movement' but fail to accompany said movement with 'Thought'. The result is a dull blade. Because the trainee hasn't thought their way through said movements, they haven't been able to finely hone or sharpen its edge. Sure a dull edge is better than no edge, but wouldn't you rather have the sharpest blade? Traditional Dry-Fire systems also focus on one movement, 'Trigger Presses', and completely fail to incorporate all the other components of Firearms Combatives, like Stance, Grip, Proper Alignment, Follow-Through, Loading & Re-Loading etc. In order to master Firearms Combatives, one must understand the relationship between 'Thought' and 'Kinesis' and amalgamate these into the mastery of the overall use of their firearm.

When you watch a Japanese Aikido master practice his craft, it looks much like a slow-motion choreographed dance. The reason is because he's learned the magic of marrying thought to movement. When I say 'Thought', I mean laser focused, Zen like concentration. When I say 'Movement' I mean a sloth like slow-motion, over exaggerated, individual and precise sequence of multiple variances. The Aikido warrior becomes a 'Master' of his craft by perfecting the art of 'Thinking Through' his movement's in training, so as to develop a surgically lethal orchestra of combative movement, strategically constructed to embody a given Combative Response for tomorrow's fight. Like a slug on a trail, the Master perfects their art by breaking-down the individual actions of an overall physical response, into minute forms of movement. They then go about polishing each and every individual process to arrive at a perfectly performed kinesthetic response.

To understand this better let's, explore the Japanese concept of 'Kata' which means 'Form' or in other words a particular 'From' of a physical discipline. In Japanese Martial Arts, they believe each physical discipline tells a story and each story can be choreographed into a slow-motion dance and with that dance, one can train to 'Master' their discipline.

Kata is based on (3) very important understandings:

1. The 'Structural Integrity' of that discipline.
2. The, 'Coherence' and relationship of the movements required for that discipline.
3. The overall 'Intent' behind that specific discipline.

In terms of Structural Integrity, this discipline is broken up in to a multitude of individually unique movements. Some of these movements are big, while others are small, some of them simple while others are much more complicated, some can be performed quickly while other must be done slowly and with consistent momentum. In the end, the combination of these movements and their orientation to one another, must make sense and one movement must be applicable with the next.

In terms of the Coherence of these movements, everything must flow together to appear to be, one seamless and perfectly performed action. Like water poured from a cup, each individual molecule must be perfectly adhered to the next so that from the outside, it appears the action of fighting is so perfectly complete and intact, that it resembles a cup of water's ability to be poured; which consists of millions of individual water molecules all falling, melding together to fall to the ground as 'One', at the same speed and in the same fashion.

The Intent of the discipline at hand, speaks for itself. Oddly when it relates to Firearms Self-Defense training, 99% of the methods in existence, completely ignore this all important component. The obvious intent is to 'Kill' your enemy before they kill you. The cognition of the concept of 'Killing' is completely absent at almost every firearms range known to man. Don't get me wrong, most people fully understand the end goal will likely result in someone's death, but the actual cognitive process of the 'Thought' of killing, while practicing each individual movement of shooting, is as foreign a concept as Pluto is to Mercury, on most ranges. By focusing on the intent behind the craft while training, knowing that each and every minute movement pertains to the 'Action' of 'Killing' your Threat and that the ability to 'Kill' your Threat is, completely dependent upon the combination of the overall Structural Integrity of your action and its cohesive qualities to each particular movement, requires one to take their training to a whole new level of consciousness. Its only then that a person is able to 'Master' their Combative Response through the management of their movements.

It is this art form, which enables someone to become a master of the craft of Firearms Self-Defense. While other training methods fall short, the *ZuluFight Dry-Fire Training System* is founded on the concept of 'Kata' and is the most balanced approach capable of unthinkable levels of proficiency. It's been painstakingly design to incorporate all aspects of firearms use. Through a Zen like attention to detail, the ZuluFighter is able to polish each and every aspect of firearms use, from the draw, it's presentation, manipulation, loading and reloading, malfunction mitigation, carry and shooting positions, from standing or even seated, standing idle and even moving as well as After Action Scanning techniques. There's nothing like it on the market, it's inexpensive, is performed when and where you'd like, requires no trips to the range and is the fastest way to achieve the highest level of firearms proficiency possible. It truly is a Firearms Total Training System. *ZuluFight* is a must have, an investment you simply can't go without. Turn to Page 173 to learn more about this must have system.

Stress inoculation...

Your next step in towards the development of the most squared away Self-Defense Response, is to prepare your mind for the battle ahead. The famed tactician Sun Tzu tells us to win our battles a thousand times before we ever face our enemies. When you delve into the logic behind such a simple approach to victory, you quickly understand just how daunting the task of 'Winning' actually is.

Sun Tzu realized that no matter how 'Powerful' you may be today, conflict itself has a way of wearing down even the most experienced warrior tomorrow. He fully understood the realities associated with battle, realizing that there are a number of Psychological and Physiological effects, which simply can't be avoided and which directly work against your chances of success. However, he also understood the gift of 'Strategy' and how pre-planning or war-rooming, can exponentially increase one's ability to win in spite of the odds.

In order to overcoming tomorrows torrent of stress, you must immerse yourself in the world of 'Force Science'. Force Science is the study of conflict and its effect on the human body both physically and psychologically. This is by far the MOST overlooked aspect of battle prepping for both the citizen and professional alike. I can't stress the importance of learning all you can today about what WILL happen tomorrow. In fact, I've dedicated a whole section on the subject of Force Science. You are encouraged to read and reread that section as much as possible. Gaining a solid grasp of the concepts of Force Science will afford you the Sea Legs you'll need tomorrow, when the apocalyptic tsunami; called Combat Stress, surges over you, soaking you through and through. There are ways to reinforce your foundations today, so you can weather the storm and survive the battle ahead. However, doing so requires your diligence right now, in learning and preparing yourself for the whirlwind of chaos you will face when your life is threatened.

After you've submerged yourself in the concepts of Force Science, it's time to go about inoculating yourself ahead of time. As previously mentioned, there are a number of psychological and physiological affects you will experience in Combat, which simply can't be avoided. However, there are things you can do today, to limit their effect so you can better manage the experience of them tomorrow. The best way to do this is through Force on Force scenario based training.

One of the best examples of Force on Force training can be found on the First Person Defender YouTube page. First Person Defender is a company who offers realistic Self-Defense scenario based training opportunities, which are completely free to the YouTube viewer. What makes their video's such a powerful asset, is that each scenario is played real-time from multiple camera angles, giving you the feeling of being right there, while also allowing for that third-person, outside looking in perspective. On top of this, each scenario is also debriefed and critiqued in-depth, allowing you the

opportunity to learn a plethora of lessons from each and every scenario.

Force on Force training allows you the ability to see and feel the effects of Combat before the battle actually occurs. Because the roll-player is forced into a stressfully combative environment, requiring their need to make lightning quick decisions with accuracy, while also implementing an instantaneous Self-Defense Response, this experience is etched deep into their psyche. The byproduct of this etching affords your subconscious brain an ability to memorize the 'Experience' of conflict. Even though Force on Force training is, training and not a real-life fight, the level of stress is such that after only a few exposures to this type of training, a novice can quite easily approach a similar real-world occurrence with not only confidence, but with an unconscious awareness and knowhow for tomorrow's battle.

You are greatly encouraged to not only view each First Person Defender scenario, but to actually seek-out this training for yourself. Even if you attend only one class, you'll walk away light-years ahead of the game. What most people do is seek range based Tactical course. They do so with the full expectation that at least a portion of the training, will be retained and later used should their lives actually be threated. Unfortunately, until you're 'Brain' has experienced some sort of Force on Force scenario incorporating what you've learned on the range, you WON'T employ those tactics tomorrow. That is unless you have the time and money to send every day for three years, attending high-speed tactical training like a Navy SEAL. In which case your 'Brain' would have found a way to etch said training for an instantaneous response tomorrow. Trust me, you NEED to attend as many Force on Force classes as possible. Take the time and invest the money.

Another way to inoculate yourself for tomorrow's battle is by adopting a 'What When Mentality'. Don't settle for a passive; "If this happens, then I'll do that" type of approach for tomorrow's attack. Instead, develop an adherence to the concept of, 'Not If But When.' Don't merely own a firearm for 'If' something should happen. Rather, actively possess it for WHEN your life WILL be threatened and WHEN you WILL be forced to use it, to protect yourself and someone else. It's this mindset that immediately thrusts you into a whole new world of mental preparation. I'm not suggesting you become paranoid of the world around you. However, I am compelling you to prepare for whatever WILL be thrown your way. If you prepare for the worst-case scenario and devise a few practical ways of defeating such an obstacle, then anything less than that should be easily overcome. It's a bit like resistance training. If you train yourself to lift a heavy weight, then pretty soon the lighter ones feel like feathers. The more you lift the fitter you become and the fitter you are, the more capable you are for the challenge.

The 'What When Mentality' translates into: "when I'm confronted by someone while I exit my front door" and "when I'm walking to my car in a dark parking garage and I'm attacked from behind" and "when I'm sitting on my couch and I'm startled by the front door being kicked in" and "when I'm at a stoplight and am confronted by a man with a gun at my driver side window" and "when I'm at the mall with my kids and see a man with a rifle killing people left and right" or "when out at a sports bar enjoying drinks with my friends and a stranger picks a fight with me." These are examples of the depth by which you must take your thought and for each 'When' you need to take the time to formulate at least three different ways of overcoming such an occurrence.

Remember, tomorrow's fight WILL be a reaction to an attack that's already underway. This means you're already behind the 8-Ball. It may also occur at ranges within arm's reach. In cases like this, you may have to either fight 'To' your weapon, or even forgo the use of your firearm altogether and settle for a hands-on defense.

Regardless, what you do today to inoculate yourself for tomorrow's unavoidable obstacles, makes all the difference.

Tactics...

One of the biggest errors people make when it comes to firearms training, is that they rely too heavily on Range based training. What I mean is they wrongly assume that by either going to a firearms range to shoot or that by attending a Range based class, that they will somehow walk away a more capable fighter. Sadly, they couldn't be more wrong. I've trained side-by-side with countless individuals, who underwent the very same high-speed, low-drag, uber sexy tactical schools as I, and seen them freeze in the face of a real fight.

Just because you've attended some cool training, and just because you were the star trainee who walked away with the highest scores, doesn't mean you're ready for tomorrow. Unless your tactical training is based and built upon the previous mentioned foundation of Firearms Kata and Stress Inoculation, you're doomed for failure and all you're doing is wasting valuable time and money.

What you should do is spend the time to build a solid foundation of understanding. Then reinforce that foundation by conditioning your body and mind to Master the tools you plan on bring to the battle. It's not until you've gained a high level of proficiency in the actual use; or shall I say manipulation, of your weapon, that actual Range based training becomes useful.

Once you have gained an acceptable level of proficiency and can, load, unload, clear malfunctions and manipulate your trigger without having to stop and think about what to do, then it's time to seek actual 'Tactical Training'. There are a ton of so called 'Experts' out there. Do your homework and don't just settle on one, find a two or three instructors who know what they're talking about. There is power in diversity of training, it makes that 'Edge' even sharper and gives you multiple trains of thought to overcome the same problem.

Section 12
What is Force Science?

Force Science is the study of the most extreme forms of physical conflict between humans known as 'Deadly Force Encounters'. Force Science dissects the dynamics associated with Combat to identify and measure physiological and psychological effects, which may be common from one person to another.

Force Science is a frailly new discipline, which began in the early 1970s. The intent was twofold:

1. The Special Operations Community wanted to find ways to increase a warfighters' overall potency on the battlefield and identify ways to pass this on to the regular army.

2. Top military brass were concerned with the overwhelming number of service members returning from Vietnam, who suffered from extreme psychological disorders. The extremely high numbers of Psych Casualties were most alarming and far greater than any previous conflict. They wanted to figure out what if anything had changed; in terms of Combat, and exactly how Combat; itself, effected the average warfighter.

The long and short is that scientists found exactly what they were searching for, but they also uncovered a treasure trove of information that's completely changed how we approach Combat today. However, it took some time for scientist, psychologist and doctors to catch up to a whole new way of thinking.

Twenty years later; in the 1990s, two main groups took this research to a whole new level and made it the science we know today. KILLOLOGY RESEARCH GROUP and the FORCE SCIENCE INSTITUTE ® are two completely independent and unbiased-based groups comprised of scientists, doctors, psychologist and tactical experts, who focus on the physiological and psychological effects of Deadly Force Encounters. Man has been in Combat since Cane and Able, yet astonishingly, the 'Science' behind Combat has been pretty much hit and miss, (pun intended) until the advent of the above mentioned groups.

They were the first to connect the dots and fill in the gaps from the more archaic research of the 1970s. They were able to identified patterns and extrapolate probable outcomes to give us a much better understand of exactly what to expect when we're faced with a deadly threat. What their research has found tells us that we've been doing it wrong all along. Sadly, we've been training to LOSE not to win.

Combat Gravity...

If there is one thing the study of Force Science has revealed, it would be that there exists a myriad of unavoidable and common effects, which everybody experiences. Combat itself has a very distinct impact on how a person will actually physically respond while threatened. This impact is vastly different than how a person acts under ANY other circumstances, other than during the most extreme life or death situations. The sum of these effects represent what I call the 'Laws of Combat'. These laws can be likened to Sir Isaac Newton's 'Laws of Physics'. The mere existence of Combat, has a measurable and defined effect on man. Regardless of race, nationality, gender or physical composition, there are a handful of common effects of Combat, which cannot be averted.

Think of it in terms of 'Gravity'. Everybody knows the effect of gravity when it relates to our ability to maneuver here on Earth. It's what keeps our feet to the ground, our constant. In the same way, Combat has its own gravitational force. There are physiological and psychological realties that affect every man, woman or child who experiences Combat.

The reality is that we all experience extremely similar effects during a struggle for our existence. While each individual effect is not guaranteed, every human being engaged in Combat, will experience the majority of them to one extreme or another. While these effects are completely unavoidable, their influence can be dramatically reduced to a much more manageable degree. Science has shown that we can pre-condition our minds and in turn our bodies; beforehand, to experience 'Combat Gravity' with less overall effect on our ability to navigate its waters.

An analogy of this concept can be derived from the conditioning an Astronaut undergoes prior to their travel into outer space. Over a life of experiencing the effects of Gravity here on Earth, their bodies have developed their own harmonic balance. If abruptly thrust into space and placed on the Moon, a person would experience great discomfort and fear without proper preparation, since they would end up bouncing from one side to the other. To this day Astronauts practice simulated Low Gravity Training, so they're adequately prepared for the effects of said Gravity on the Moon or Space in general. Something as simple as drinking water in Space, can be a very daunting task and extremely difficult to complete while in Space. Yet on Earth this most basic function, which most of us master by the age of (4), is taken for granted here on Earth. Similar basic physical functions associated with using a firearm while under attack, are just as much an out-of-this-world experience as drinking water from a cup, in an almost zero gravity environment like that of the International Space Station.

Just as the Moon is a world away from our experiences here on Earth, Combat is as distant our everyday lives as Mars or better yet Pluto. In the same way, Force Science has shown that anyone can prep for tomorrow's battle and develop natural responses to afford them the most positive outcome.

An example on how poor training can completely sabotage one's ability to win during the 'Act' of Combat, can be found in something as simple as how they stand during training. Stance is one of the most overlooked aspects of firearms training, yet it provides the entire base for your Physical Response. For the most part people initially acquire a stance that looks tactical cool like the 'Isosceles Stance'. But soon and usually within a few short minutes, their stance becomes more of a flat-footed, weight on heals Weaver Stance. What happens is they lose focus of the 'Crouch' and forward lean required for an effective Isosceles Stance and quickly get tired due to muscle fatigue. What results is the entirety of the rest of their training is performed from a completely different base, which completely effects overall accuracy. The laziness and poor habitual manner of their stance in training, is then encoded in their brain as Muscle Memory through the procedural aspects of their training.

Interestingly, Force Science research clearly shows that EVERYONE who actually perceives an immediately attacking lethal threat, will instinctively assume a squatted crouch, identical to that of the Modified Isosceles shooting stance. No matter how well you've training and no matter how elite your profession may be, this is latterly an innate physical reaction that CAN'T be overridden. A great example of this can be seen in the video footage of then President Reagan's attempted assassination on March 30th 1981. During this real-world deadly attack EVERY single individual is seen assuming an 'Oh Shi Crouch' directly proceeding John Hinckley Junior's initial shots.

What's even more interesting is that each and every person immediately present did the same exact thing regardless of their previous training or their current physical responsibility. From reporter, to staff, to regular police officers to the elite team of Reagan's Secret Service Detail, each and every person crouched and maintained that crouch throughout their following Physical Response. Remember, members of a Secret Serve Presidential Security Detail, undergo a degree of unheard of pre-training and continued training that could easily be likened to the practice of a Religion. Even with all their training, each Secret Service member crouched in the same fashion and even paused for about the same amount of time, prior to putting into motion their Defensive Response.

The reality is that during attack you WILL assume a 'Modified Isosceles Stance' throughout the incident regardless of your previous training. If Force Science has proven that this is as much of a reality as Gravity is to the Law of Physics, then why do so many people waste so much time shooting from a Weaver or any other type of shooting stance? Your shooting stance is your 'Base' it determines and galvanizes the overall integrity of all other aspects of fighting which shooting is but 'One' portion. Maintaining proper stance through the entirety of your training will assure that all the other physical movements you hone during that training evolution, are not wasted and are built on a sure foundation that's consistent with the Laws of Combat and don't attempt to defy the Laws of Physics. Understanding something so simple yet so vitally important as 'Stance' during training, highlights just why an adequate grasp of the topic of Force Science is so essential if you want to 'Win' tomorrow's battle. Winning is first accomplished through the 'pre'-study of conflict.

The mind, a terrible thing to waste...

Our brains define us and set us apart from all other living beings. The totality, function and overall capabilities they offer are inconceivable. Neuroscientists are still uncovering the secrets and wonder behind how our brains develop and function. Our brains are truly our greatest asset. Yet, in times of great crisis they can often become our greatest obstacle.

Force Science researchers have consistently shown that our ability to manage 'Combat Stress' is directly derived from how our minds process the concepts of this stress beforehand. It's all about pre-conditioning. In fact, our success is completely dependent upon our mind's ability to formulate an instantaneous response absent cognitive thought. Just as our brain's continually cause our lungs to expand and contract without thought, so too must we have a pre-wired solution for tomorrow's battle. This starts by understanding the processes of our physiology and psychology and how they're affected during Combat. Similar to how an Olympic Athlete utilizes Hyperbaric Chamber Training to pre-condition their lungs for the extreme stressors of such a high level of competition, so too must you pre-condition the physiology and psychology of your mind for Combat.

Fight, Flight or Freeze...

Over the course of our lives, our brains have subconsciously developed one of three instantaneous responses to an immediate and deadly threat. We will either 'Fight' our Threat with all our might, 'Flee' from it as fast as humanly possible or we will completely shut down and 'Freeze' like a deer caught in the headlights. This is also known as 'Combat Paralysis', which can last anywhere from seconds or minutes and can easily lead to a medical state of shock.

Our brains are designed to develop and operate on two parallel planes. During times of grave danger and when faced with a threat to our very existence, our brains revert back to the most primitive forms of function.

1. The most common plane, I like to call the 'Intelligent Brain'. It's where we live 99.99% of our lives. It's the cognitive and intellectually creative form of us. This operation is achieved through the cooperative interaction of our Prefrontal Cortex with both our brain's right and left hemispheres.

    - To better understand this, our Intelligent Brain is like our desktop computer. It's comprised of all that makes our computer different than the next. It is made up of its operating system and background functions, the main hard-drive, auxiliary drives and the multitude of custom software suites.

2. The more primitive plane is much different than our Intelligent Brain. I call this the 'Caveman Brain' or the Amygdala. It's mainly comprised of all our basic body functions; the innate processes our brain makes on its own, which maintain all 11 basic body function systems, like those of our nervous and circulatory

systems. It also consists of an extremely small sampling of our Intelligent Brain's ability to problem solve.

- To better understand this, our Caveman Brain is like our desktop computer's master default, the archaic DOS or C Prompt. No Windows OS, no software, just code.

- Many so called Tactical Experts have training methods which fall apart during real-life Combat because they designed their methods on an Intellectual footing requiring the use of one's 'Intelligent' cognitive brain function. However, during the polar shift of Combat; where our brains revert back to Caveman function, all those 'Intellectual' possesses go out the window. In Combat you're left with basic computer code, while all those fancy dancy high-tech tactical sexy software applications end up crashing. What you should be doing is learning to be a Combat Computer IT Analyst because that's exactly what you'll need when someone tries to kill you tomorrow and you're faced with the complexities of the unavoidable Combat Computer Code Crash.

Due to genetics and early childhood influences, our Caveman Brains accumulate a mixture of automated responses which are immediately fired when faced with grave danger. This is that small sampling of intellectual problem solving discussed above. When faced with a problem our Caveman Brain throws an extremely primitive solution at it. It really is basic Addition & Subtraction though; it's nowhere near the level of Trigonometry or even Basic Algebra. These automated, pre-programmed, responses are completely innate and instinctive. They're an instantaneous function requiring almost zero cognitive processing whatsoever.

Similar to our body's homeostasis; how it regulates and maintains the perfect PH balance, our brains develop their own form of psychoneuro-homeostasis. Over a lifelong of external influences and experiences, our brains establish a physiological and physiological balance. When balanced, this state of being enables our Intelligent Brains to function with ease in relation to the world around us. However, when faced with impending death, this balance is violently thrown upside-down. At that moment our Caveman Brain floods our systems with a cocktail of the most potent hormones and chemicals. The effects of this mind altering chemical cocktail greatly affects our body's response to the perceived Threat and ultimately determines our overall ability to respond to the Threat(s) or whether we Fight, Flee or end-up Freeze.

Top Secret...

When faced with a deadly threat to our very existence, our brains feverishly search for a folder titled 'Top Secret'. This folder holds the solution to our immediate problem. The trouble arises when our brains experiences the polar shift; mentioned previously, as it goes from using the Intelligent Brain to our primitive Caveman Brain. It's at that moment when our secretary; our brain's Amygdala, grabs the first folder she can get her hands on and throws it at the problem. The probability that she will retrieve the particular individual folder, which contains your specifically tailored solution for that particular problem, is completely dependent upon how you've already organized, correlated and filed that folder beforehand. When it comes to the use of a weapon in response to an attacking threat; how you respond, is completely dependent upon the degree and quality of Procedural Memory Encoding you've performed beforehand.

Our brains are like huge storage vaults capable of storing a life's long accumulation of information and experiences. For the most part we organize these banks of information in similar fashion to that of a filing system. For Combat experts, this system is as sophisticated as the vault like industrial catalogs like those you'd find at a courthouse or museum.

Most people however, file their information in a much less technical manner. This would more closely resemble an everyday two drawer filing cabinet. Over time our brains develop habits of storage, utilizing different kinds of coding and correlating. Some folders are red while others are blue. Some folders go to the top drawer while others live in the bottom. Some are situated to the left while others are stored to the right. In an everyday world; while experience everyday experiences with low stress, your Intelligent Brain can typically locate nearly any folder by memory of where it was last stored. This is due to the process of Cognitive Thought, which is the brain's overall cooperative effort of all its parts.

Ninety-nine point nine-nine percent of Westerners live their lives in an ultra-state of peace. In fact, most Westerners will go a lifetime without being physically confronted let alone have someone actually try and kill them. It's important to understand this because just as our Intelligent Brain develops habits of process, our Caveman Brain does as well. The brain is a muscle and like any muscle, if it's not used, it becomes weak. The down side to our peace filled lives is that our Caveman Brain hardly if ever gets its workout in. So when death comes knocking, our Amygdala is left with the daunting task of finding that 'One' perfect solution for an out-of-this-world problem, amongst the clutter of all the other files, piled up around her. This is where the right kind of training makes all the difference and is precisely why the 'Right' kind of training is so essential.

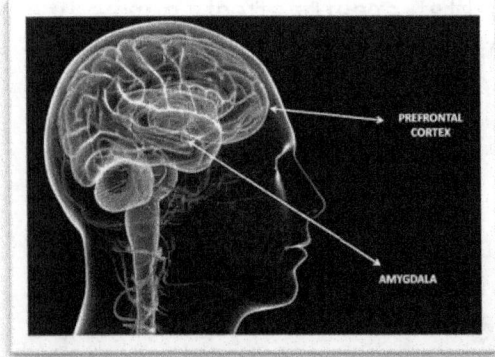

Our Intelligent Brain utilizes the vastness of the Prefrontal Cortex; which is about the size of your fist, to calculate its solutions for the world around it. In contrast, our Caveman Brain uses an area the size of a pea, the Amygdala. That tiny, barely legible portion of the otherwise vastness of the rest of our brain, that's what our Caveman Brain uses to formulate its response to a Deadly Encounter. That tiny, insignificant dot is the most significantly momentous apparatuses in your entire body. This is what <u>WILL</u> determine how you respond to deadly threats. Placing the 'Right' information in an appropriately marked folder during training and storing it in the proper spot, that's what will make all the difference tomorrow. It's this tiny portion of our brain; the Amygdala, that has become the focal point of Force Science. It's this extremely miniscule region of the human brain which gets all the attention. Your ability to overcome tomorrow's deadly threat is dependent upon how well you understand this process and how well you 'Condition' and encode a pre-programmed response. Proper conditioning is only achieved through proper training. However, it's not just about 'Training' but the 'Right' kind of training makes this possible.

Most of us place the cart before the horse. We spend a small fortune on that perfect gun, which by all means is guaranteed to stop any bad guy dead in his tracks, right? Wrong! From time to time we set out on a pilgrimage to Tactical Mecca, where we hewn and ready our hands for battle by plinking at cardboard silhouettes or even glass bottles. We then return home and go about our lives as normal. Rarely do we ever actually take the time to stop and 'Think Through' the physiology and psychology of conflict. Neurologists go to school first. Ninety-five percent of their time is spent in books and lecture halls before they ever touch a human brain, let alone begin to cut into one. The kinesis of battle is useless if your brain hasn't been conditioned in the process of selecting the appropriate Tactical Response under the extreme stresses of Combat.

Taking the time to study Force Science and memorizing the scientific Laws of Combat will pay dividends tomorrow. Learning first what your body WILL do, will save you from spending tons of wasted time at the firearms range, inadvertently conditioning and encoding the 'Wrong' tactics for the wrong response.

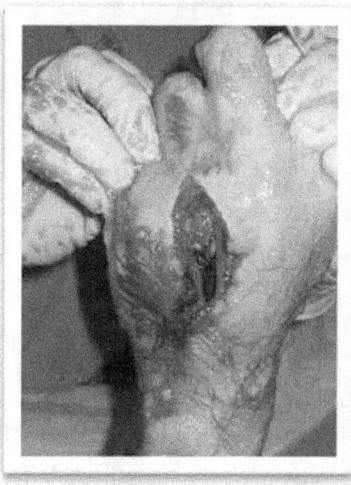

Warning Apocalyptic Tsunami Ahead!!!

What's all the hype about? What's the big deal? You're ready you say? Oh yes, because you have a 1911 .45 ACP by your side at all times. You're ready for anything....

The truth? Physical confrontations with firearms is the most fluidly dynamic environment you will ever know. The overwhelming and unavoidable tidal wave of physiological and psychological effects, rates up there with an Apocalyptic Tsunami. Armed confrontations aren't action movies or video games and they're no 3 Gun match. There are no do-overs and EVERY error is immediately accompanied by a devastatingly lethal consequence.

Most armed citizens foolishly assume they're defensive firearms abilities are suffice. Many think that because they grew-up around firearms, carry one everywhere they go or because they're an expert 3 Gun competitor; they actually believe whole heartedly, they're ready for Combat. The problem lays in their ignorance of 'Fact' and of the unavoidable troubles which lurk ahead. They simply have no clue of the deluge that will wash over them like the worst kind of tidal wave imaginable. They aren't prepared for, or even aware of, the concept of 'Combat Gravity' nor are have the conditioned themselves to react appropriately in spite of the apocalyptic effects of Combat Stress. For instance:

Action vs. Reaction:

1. The average untrained attacker can achieve a (90%) hit ratio on their prey, while the average untrained defender can only achieve upwards of around a (17-20%) hit ratio in response?

2. Statistics show that 90% of real-world shootings involve multiple rounds being fired and the average untrained person can shoot (4) rounds per-second. That's right, I said an "Untrained" person can shoot (4) rounds per-second.

3. Action is ALWAYS faster than reaction, it's a scientific fact. It takes the average human (0.30) seconds to simply react to a change in their environment. That's merely identifying the existence of 'Change', NOT reacting to said change. Now begins the daunting task of 'Reaction'. Given the overwhelming Stress Cocktail associated with any deadly attack, it takes a minimum of (0.53) more seconds to overcome and process the initial shock & awe of that attack. Then after all that; at (0.83) seconds, you can actually begin to implement some type of a physical response. Meaning, it's not until (0.83) seconds into the fight that your brain tells your hand to move towards your holster.

4. Now consider the totality of the relationship between Action vs. Reaction, physics and your ability to survive the attack. The problem presented is a bad guy who's threatened or is actually using a gun against you. You're already drastically behind the Eight Ball. To survive you must identify the Threat, formulate a response, and then implement said response. As mentioned previously you're likely to sustain between (6.52 – 10.88) hits before you send your first round. If you don't believe this statistic, YouTube the 1981 President Reagan Assassination Attempt. You'll see that John Hinckley Jr. was able to get (6) rounds off, before some of the World's most highly trained and capable individuals were able to finally subdue him.

5. This real-world Deadly Encounter is a perfect example because it gives you a snapshot of the cross-section of tactically minded persons present, from the horribly inept reporters and advisors and press sectaries to the elite of the elite Secret Service Presidential Detail members. It took each of these people so much time to respond that John Hinckley Jr. was able to shoot (6) times in (1.7) seconds, standing (10) feet away from President Reagan. His first shot was a headshot of all things. Four of his (6) shots hit multiple people including Reagan all before he could be subdued. It's only certain Reagan would have been hit more would he not have had an entourage of people immediately present to protect his life. You can rest assure, you WON'T have a Secret Service Detail protecting you when you're attacked.

6. Remerging that bullets don't discriminate between right or wrong, friend or foe, victim or criminal, the reality is that molten hot, razor-sharp, metal objects will likely tare through your body at nearly 1,200 fps. This will cause profuse bleeding and immediately begin the ultimate shutdown of the majority of your overall bodily functions. It's only after this, that science shows that you're humanly capable to draw your weapon and begin the uphill battle of defending your life. Does that concern you? Does it make your stomach turn? It most certainly should. This is why the 'Right' kind of training makes all the difference beforehand.

Close Quarters Battles (C.Q.B.) / Proximity to Threat:

1. Distance equals time. The shorter the distance the less time one has to perceive an attack, react and then overcome the perceived deadly attack.

2. Distance also affects accuracy. Since you're reacting to attack, proximity is NOT your friend. The closer your Threat is, the less accurate he needs to be to achieve lethal hits. If your Threat is completely inept at 25 yards and couldn't even place one round on paper, at two or three feet, it's entirely possible that he'll score a possible and each of his rounds will rip through you before you even react.

3. At close proximity a number of other factors are immediately present. For instance, you can touch, feel, smell and even taste your Threat. The aroma of his body odor, the clamminess of his skin, the perplexing and paralyzing gaze of his lifeless thousand-yard stare. An up close and personal struggle for life with another human being is simply unmatched. It's daunting, spooky and emotionally unsettling even for the most experienced among us.

The Stress Cocktail:

5. **Fear (The Human Phobia of Death):** The greatest most unavoidable innate reaction to a deadly threat is our natural fear of death. While some can learn to dilute and decrease the effect of this reaction, most people will be thrust into a whirlwind of paralyzing fear. Lt. Col. Dave Grossman coined it "The Human Phobia of Death." Like any of our most extreme phobias; spiders, snakes or heights, our entire being will immediately be galvanized. It will be like getting struck by lightning. Potent chemicals and hormones, like adrenalin and dopamine, will flood our bloodstream. The effects of which will throw your brain into an ultra DEFCON 1 level of security lockdown. From here, only the bodily functions required to perceive the Threat, determine an immediate response and then react to said Threat, will function. Everything else goes on lockdown. You simply revert back to the Caveman Brain where the only thing that matters is survival. It's at this moment that you will either Fight, Flee or Freeze. Sadly, most freeze, bring unavoidable death.

6. **Heart Rate Explosion:** An adults normal resting heart rate lives anywhere between (60-80) bpm. Optimal competitive function lives between (115-145) bpm. At this range you're afforded the perfect combination of blood & oxygen flow throughout your body, which enables optimal performance of your entire system. However, for the average citizen who's never faced an actual deadly attack, it's entirely possible for your heart rate to spike between (180-220) bpm or even higher. This is a very dangerous range. Even during normal everyday exercise, like running on a treadmill, if maintained over an extended period of time, this can easily cause cardiac arrest. This range is CATASTROPHIC while in heated battle. Due to the presence of the abnormally high levels of dangerous chemicals, the tidal wave of adrenalin and dopamine; which is violently pumping through you, if your heart rate isn't brought back to a safe level, cardiac arrest can occur within seconds as opposed to minutes. Even if you avoid cardiac arrest, at this range your body teeters between Conditions Gray & Black, meaning you're on the verge of total physical shutdown, like an engine seizing from a lack of oil.

7. **Loss of Peripheral Vision:** This is known as 'Focused Vision' or 'Tunnel Vision'. During attack the ONLY thing you will see is what you need to see. The color of the leaves on a distant tree, the little old lady crossing the street, or even the gigantic skyscraper standing directly behind the person trying to kill you. These are all irrelevant and will likely be completely erased from your perceived vision. This can be a good thing as it will give you a laser beam like, focused type of clarity of your Threat, but what if you're attacked by two or more individuals? Or what about when you consider your response and begin to fire back? Where are your rounds going to go should they miss? Will they hit the little old lady crossing the street? Or the family quietly eating their lunch in the restaurant directly behind your Threat?

8. Loss of Near Vision: Think about this, if you can't see your sights because your eyes simply can't see them; due to the fact that your eyes are ONLY trained on that which is trying to actively kill you, how are you going to use your sights to hit your Threat? While under attack, your eyes will see only what they need to see. Because your sights aren't trying to kill you, your eyes won't see them. Again, all your eyes car about is focusing on whomever or whatever it straying to kill you. This sort of phasing out of non-threatening objects is also true for other objects or non-treating people within the spectrum of your near vision.

9. **Loss of Depth Perception:** We rely on our ability to decipher depth in relation to our proximity to objects and surfaces around us. A drastic loss of this important sense would be like trying to fight while experiencing vertigo. Not knowing the true distance to objects in your immediate environment, increases the likelihood that you will trip or stumble, making you completely vulnerable and useless during attack. Understanding this now can help to elevate moments of panic should this occur during your fight.

10. **Auditory Exclusion:** As a result of the perceived likelihood of death, you may experience a temporary loss of hearing. Similar to 'Focused Vision', your ears will be trained on your Threat and will completely block out the plethora of sounds in your environment. A good example of this is best understood by those who've ever hunting before. When they raise their rifle and shoot their game, the report of the rifle sounds like a muffled pop-gun and their hearing is hardly affected. Yet shooting that same rifle on the range absent hearing protection would leave their ears ringing in pain. Much of this is due to the high levels of adrenaline and dopamine that will surge through your body. In a real gunfight you'll likely experience the same kinds of auditory effects, where everything but your Threat appears muffled.

11. **Loss of Fine Motor Skills:** We rely on Fine Motor Skills for everything. In many ways it's what separates us from primates. Our ability to thread a needle provides the clothing on our backs. Our ability to put thought to paper, by holding a small pen to artistically communicate thoughts and ideas on paper, affords us the ability to

expand our understanding. This fine motor skill alone; manipulating a pen to put thoughts on paper, provides blueprints of success for our children and our children's children. Our abilities to finely manipulate our bodies enables us to dominate our environment. However, while under deadly attack, your physiological system is taken out of balance and you will lose the ability to do simple physical things. Under these situations you're left with trying to force a square peg through a round hole or sinking a small nail on a wall with a 20 lb. sledgehammer.

12. **The Slow Motion Effect:** A well-known phenomenon, which effects most people who experience extreme high levels of stress during deadly attack, is perceived slow motion. Time itself appears to literally come to a halt and barely ticks by. The best way to articulate this is to compare it to the scene in the movie 'The Matrix' where Neo dodges the torrent of bullets being fired at him, while he bends backwards and manipulates his body here and there, dodging every slow moving bullet slicing through the air. Similarly, time will appear to slow so much so that your movements may appear to be a sort of out-of-body experience.

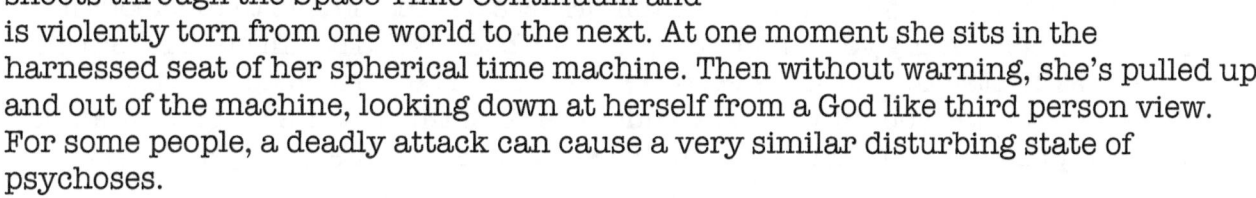

13. **The Hyper Speed Effect:** Another phenomenon is the sense that your world has just jumped into a hyper speed wormhole. Sometimes people experience a weird mixture of the two where they experience a most bewildering tug-of-war of some outside force randomly pulling them from hyper speed to slow motion and back. A good example of this is seen in the movie 'Contact' when Dr. Ellie Arroway shoots through the Space Time Continuum and is violently torn from one world to the next. At one moment she sits in the harnessed seat of her spherical time machine. Then without warning, she's pulled up and out of the machine, looking down at herself from a God like third person view. For some people, a deadly attack can cause a very similar disturbing state of psychoses.

14. **Tormenting Thoughts:** Another extremely common effect from this type of stress is an onslaught of horribly vulgar and disturbing thoughts. For some they see their life latterly pass before their eyes as if they were sitting in a movie theater; eating popcorn, while they quickly reach the climatic and tragic end of their life story. For others it's as crazy as the most exotic acid trip causing insane hallucinations. For instance, during one of my Deadly Force incidents, I swear I saw the suspect's vehicle turn into Magnetron, as it sped towards me, spilling sparks from its wheels which looked like waves of fire. A buddy of mine later explained to me that during one of his shootings, he saw a little green Leprechaun who continually taunted him throughout the gunfight telling him, "You're gonna dieeee.... You're gonna dieeee..." These kinds of psychotic trips can make it extremely difficult to maintain effective situational awareness and decipher truth from fiction.

15. **Loss of Bowel & Bladder Control:** This is probably something you never thought of when considering how you'll respond to a deadly attack on your life. The reality is our bodies will react absent cognitive thought. At that moment there is only one goal in mind, survival. Average normal bodily functions will go on lockdown, providing ample energy and blood flow for those organs which are needed to provide the essential functions to secure survival. This means if you have a full bladder or are close to passing your last meal, it's entirely possible that you will do so right then and there.

Combat Hydraulics...

Hopefully this chapter underlined the fact that Combat is the most chaotically charged, out of control, consistently fast moving environment known to man. Its hydrostatic qualities are measured in thousandths of seconds multiplied by pounds per square inch. The fluidity of this environment is as volatile as the ocean tide and as random as the ebb and flow of its surge. Sure you might be a competent swimmer in the backyard pool. Hell, you may even be able to hold your breath under water for 5-minutes. Surviving the converging surge in the Straits of Magellan; where the Atlantic and Pacific meet, without a life vest or a wetsuit, that takes a level of proficiency I'd be willing to bet you don't have and Combat is easily as tumultuous as converging oceans.

The act of defending one's self with a firearm is a daunting task even for professionals. However, Combat can be tamed. You may have zero experience and have never actually been in a fight for your life before. You're Caveman Brain my even be pre-wired to Freeze. You may actually be the worst fighter in the entire universe, but don't lose hope. There are ways to pre-condition practical lifesaving responses and encode them deep within your brain's primitive DOS / C Prompt command. There are things you can do today so you can WIN tomorrow's battle and live to tell about it. It starts here, by preparing your mind for how your body <u>WILL</u> be affected. After this you can develop kinesthetic, Tactical Responses which can be performed in spite of these effects. It's only after you fully understand these scientific realities that you can begin to develop a practical solution that actually works in a real-life gunfight.

Hopefully, this in-depth glimpse into the study of Force Science gives you the knowledge you'll need to develop both a tactical and legal response to Self-Defense. Remember, the vast majority of people haven't a clue about these realities and this includes the Judge, Jury and even your attorney. It's up to you to make this an integral part of your Defense strategy, so you can educate those involved and assure that you're not left being wrongly convicted for something that's completely out of your control.

Section 13
Preemptive Legal Defense

Regardless of whether you find yourself in Criminal or Civil Court, your ability to accurately describe exactly why you chose to do what you did is paramount. It's just as vitally important that you eliminate any chance of misunderstanding whatsoever. It's essential that your reasons for said actions are completely understood so as to be found 'Objectively Reasonable' and not simply Subjective by nature. This requires a degree of articulation that most people simply do not have and that can usually only be accomplished through the assistance of an experienced attorney.

Perspectives of Self-Defense are based on conjuncture. Conjuncture is a kaleidoscope of random yet similar assumptions of an outcome that's based on a thought process of past experiences. Perspectives are also composed of an intangible premonition of impending doom due to exposure of the knowledge of similar previous incidents, all woven together to formulate the facts by which you justified such an extreme action. So, your attorney must fully comprehend the gravity and temperature of your past experiences; whether those experiences actually happened to you or in circumstances where you're basing said actions on a someone else's real-life incident. Then they go about measuring the legality of your actions, so as to determine the best ways to formulate the most accurate explanation to the Court. They do so by selecting the 'Exact' vernacular which BEST describes your Defense.

So how do you do this? How does one explain why they did what they did when you don't even know what particular words best define it? You could wait until you've already acted in Self-Defense. You could attempt at that time and while under the most extreme amounts stress, quickly and off-the-cuff, think back to your past experiences and things you've learned. Then verbally describe those concepts to your attorney, while drawing context to the incident in question. This is what most people do but it's far from the most accurate. Sure you may remember particular things of importance, but having the ability to combine it all together so it's presentable and palatable in Court, is an entirely different story all together.

What this system provides is a means of preemptively communicating these facts to your attorney, to afford you the BEST chances of obtaining the most solid legal advice and services, customized to your particular individual needs, without being required to actively think back and remember things from say five, ten or even twenty years in the past. This manual is also specifically designed to give you the most practical means of retaining important data of similar incidents that happened to someone else, which may later actually play an active role in your decision process. *ZuluShield* also provides a similar way of retaining these incidents of Self-Defense, which Courts have previously found to be reasonable. This way you don't have to remember minute facts, times, places or even people involved, all those years later while under enormous stress. All you have to do is flip through your convenient and strategically structured *ZuluShield Archive*.

Let's revisit the Home Invasion Robbery scenario from earlier. Remember the assailant breaks in your residence in the middle of the night and you're startled from your stupor. You decide to grab your firearm and clear your house, when you confront the assailant who's standing in your living room. You're scared and can't see if he's armed or not, decide to shoot and in turn kill him. You determined your course of action for a number of reasons:

1. The person unlawfully entered and is remaining in your home.

2. Its night so you conclude that he must have assumed you'd be home, which means he would have reasonably planned for you being there and although you can't see a weapon, you believe it reasonable under those circumstances that he would have armed himself.

3. You also decided to shoot based on the fact that you know Home Invasion Robberies to be extremely dangerous and unpredictable.

4. You chose NOT to warn or tell the intruder to 'Freeze' because you know from training that 'Action' is always faster than 'Reaction' and you FEARED that by giving the intruder any more time to contemplate an attack, WOULD cost you your life.

5. Now let's say you've come to this conclusion because of a number of incidents in the past which you've seen or read about in the News and one in particular stood out, which you end up specifically siting.

All of this is mixed together and clearly articulates a reasonable basis for your actions and that you reasonably feared that your life and your family's were in grave danger and you were justified in the use of Deadly Physical Force to protect 'Life'. In no time, you're able to give clear articulation supported by tangible facts. Now contrast that with a 'Reactive Defense Strategy' where you're left picking up the pieces while you develop your Defense on-the-fly.

"That's good!" you say, "that's what I want!" Yes, the above mentioned rundown of articulation is wonderful and will undoubtedly keep you out of jail. However, for Court purposes you need much, much more. You need hard facts, something tangible, otherwise its mere conjecture and is far too 'Subjective' by nature. In Court you must present factual detail. The Court needs to know the dates and times of those past incidents you've eluded to as part of your decision process for using force. You must also show why any of that actually relates to the context of your particular Self-Defense claim. Trying to remember all this information and the overwhelming amount of other important facts, all while under the gauntlet of extreme stress, is an uphill battle and the reason why so many people fail so miserably in Court and exactly why they either plead or settle Civilly despite their innocence.

ZuluShield is specifically designed to make your Court proceedings a much easier and more successful experience. With this system you'll not only learn how to effectively articulate example after example, but your attorney will have those examples right there at their fingertips, all strategically organized to give you a bulletproof Legal Defense. Your due diligence today, will pay dividends tomorrow.

A proactive approach to tomorrow's legal battle is your only hope for success. Learn why *ZuluShield* is Firearms Legal Defense made easy. Discover the secrets you need to know today to protect against future legal action. Turn to Page 175 to learn how you can start protecting yourself today.

Section 14
Loading & ReLoading

Praise the Lord and pass the ammunition! If you survive a gun battle, you'll be doing a lot of praising the Lord. However, first you need to win that fight and ammunition is vital to that end. Feeding and keeping your firearm fed, is an essential component in winning a gunfight. As we've already discussed, most gunfights involve the expenditure of multiple rounds. If you're wise, you'll carry one or two extra loaded magazines. The idea is that you're expecting the worst case scenario, like an Active shooter / Active Threat situation or even a Terrorist Act. Regardless, you've planed a way to stay in the fight and a practical surplus of ammunition is the best way to do this. Your level of proficiency with loading and reloading, should be as simple as clapping your hands. The best way to master this, is through repetitive training and the ZuluFight Dry-Fire Training System, is the most effective way to accomplish this task. Be sure to secure your copy. Dedicate some time to mastering your reloads, so you're ready for that worst case scenario.

Loading:

Loading your semi-auto handgun is as easy as 1, 2, 3. Simply insert a loaded magazine into the magazine well located in the grip of your handgun. Then slap the bottom of the magazine to assure it's properly seated. Finally rack the slide to chamber a round and you're ready to go.

To Properly Load Do The Following:

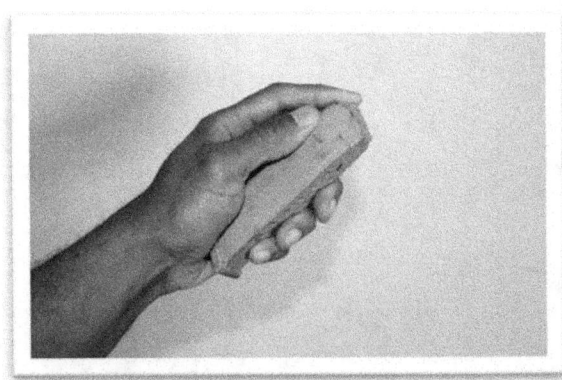

NOTE: Stage index finger on business end of Snap-Cap. This allows for more consistent loading while also assuring Snap-Cap is in correct position.

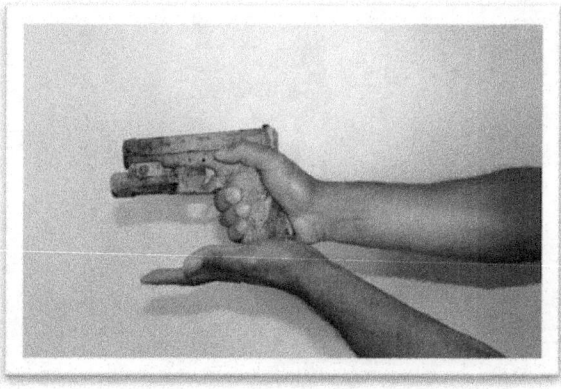

NOTE: Firmly and generously tap the bottom of the magazine to assure it is properly seated.

NOTE: Get into the habit of sweeping ejection port while obtaining grip of your slide when attempting to rack. This allows your brain to encode one solid movement for both Type 2 Malfunction clearing and normal racking.

NOTE: ALWAYS obtain an over-handed firm grip towards rear of slide. Assure finger is outside trigger guard. Push forward with gun hand while pulling back with support hand to rack slide.

NOTE: Release grip of slide after pulling it all the way to the rear. Allow slide to slam forward on its own while also allowing support hand to naturally fling back towards chest. This assures your first round will properly load.

Combat Reload:

A Combat Reload is what's needed when your gun goes dry during a gunfight. Most semi-auto firearms will lock back and stay open, to indicate that its mouth is open and ready to be fed. To feed it simply depress the magazine release, strip the empty magazine, retrieve a new one and repeat the previous mentioned loading sequence to get back into the fight.

To Perform A Proper Combat Reload Do The Following:

NOTE: Start by slightly canting firearm to allow for visual inspection of ejection port to identify stoppage. Also bring arms back allowing elbows to naturally rest on upper abdomen. This creates a natural working platform to work from allowing you to focus on your Threat while placing firearm in direct focal plane to allow you to still see your firearm utilizing peripheral vision.

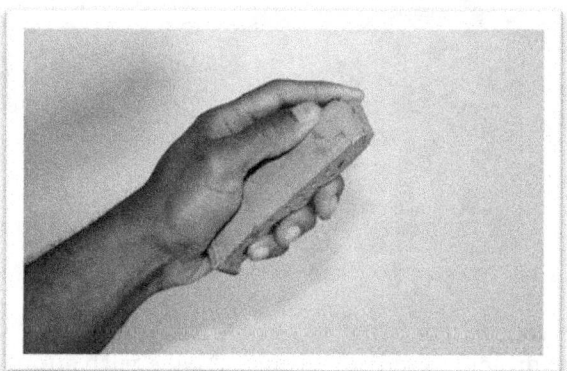

NOTE: Retrieve and Stage index finger on business end of Snap-Cap. This allows for more consistent loading while also assuring Snap-Cap is in correct position.

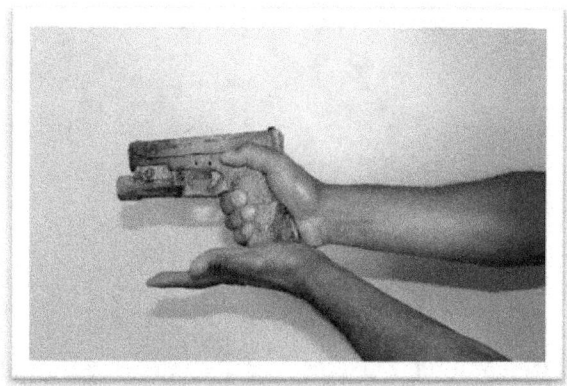

NOTE: Firmly and generously tap the bottom of the magazine to assure it is properly seated.

NOTE: Get into the habit of sweeping ejection port while obtaining grip of your slide when attempting to rack. This allows your brain to encode one solid movement for both Type 2 Malfunction clearing and normal racking.

NOTE: ALWAYS obtain an over-handed firm grip towards rear of slide. Assure finger is outside trigger guard. Push forward with gun hand while pulling back with support hand to rack slide.

NOTE: Release grip of slide after pulling it all the way to the rear. Allow slide to slam forward on its own while also allowing support hand to naturally fling back towards chest. This assures your first round will properly load.

Tactical Reload:

This is a reload performed during a tactical lull in the battle. The intent of a Tactical Reload is to top-up your firearm with more food, just in case the battle continues.

To Perform A Proper Tactical Reload Do The Following:

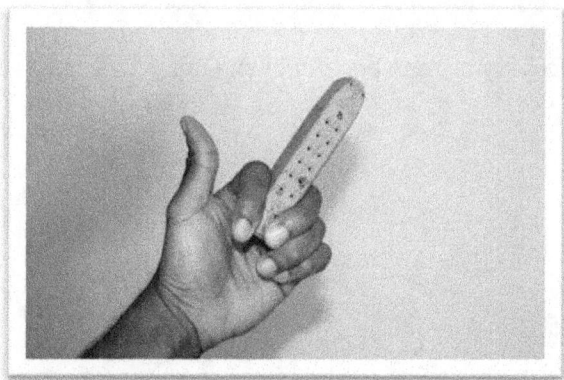

NOTE: Stage magazine so business end is faced away from body. Obtain grip at bottom of magazine placing it between index and middle finger while opening and extending thumb.

NOTE: Remove simulated partial magazine from firearm first by placing it in web of thumb. Then insert simulated fresh magazine.

NOTE: Firmly and generously tap the bottom of the magazine to assure it is properly seated.

Section 15
Malfunction Mitigation

Malfunctions are an inevitable occurrence and something you NEED to prepare for. Since you're training for a fight, it's extremely important to understand its dynamics. One of those happens to be firearms malfunctions. They can occur for a number of reasons. During a fight though, the top (3) reasons have to do with either physical contact with your Threat or yaw effect due to extreme movement or failing to apply proper grip while firing. There are (3) basic types of malfunctions and (1) Catastrophic occurrence. The forth is a mechanical failure rendering your firearm useless. While this is rare, it does occur, which is why you would also need to know other means of Self-Defense such as Krav Maga.

Type 1 Malfunction:

A Type 1 Malfunction is the most basic. There are two kinds of Type 1 Malfunctions:

- A misfire
- Slide closes on empty chamber

A misfire typically occurs because of either a poor round or damaged firing-pin. The second Type 1 typically occurs during the course of shooting, when the shooter accidently engages the magazine release and the magazine falls out of battery thereby preventing the next round from entering the chamber.

To Fix A Type 1 Malfunction Do The Following:

NOTE: Start by slightly canting firearm to allow for visual inspection of ejection port to identify stoppage. Also bring arms back allowing elbows to naturally rest on upper abdomen. This creates a natural working platform to work from allowing you to focus on your Threat while placing firearm in direct focal plane to allow you to still see your firearm utilizing peripheral vision.

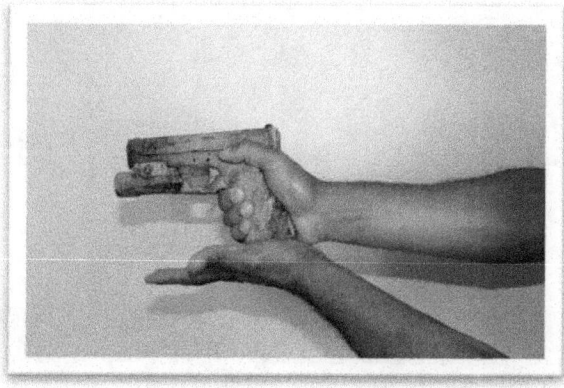

NOTE: Firmly and generously tap the bottom of the magazine to assure it is properly seated.

NOTE: Get into the habit of sweeping ejection port while obtaining grip of your slide when attempting to rack. This allows your brain to encode one solid movement for both Type 2 Malfunction clearing and normal racking.

NOTE: ALWAYS obtain an over-handed firm grip towards rear of slide. Assure finger is outside trigger guard. Push forward with gun hand while pulling back with support hand to rack slide.

NOTE: Release grip of slide after pulling it all the way to the rear. Allow slide to slam forward on its own while also allowing support hand to naturally fling back towards chest. This assures your first round will properly load.

Type 2 Malfunction:

A Type 2 Malfunction is easily identified by the spent casing which hangs from the ejection port. This is the most common malfunction in Combat situations due to a constantly changing shooting position. This typically occurs from yaw due to extreme movement or failing to apply proper grip while shooting.

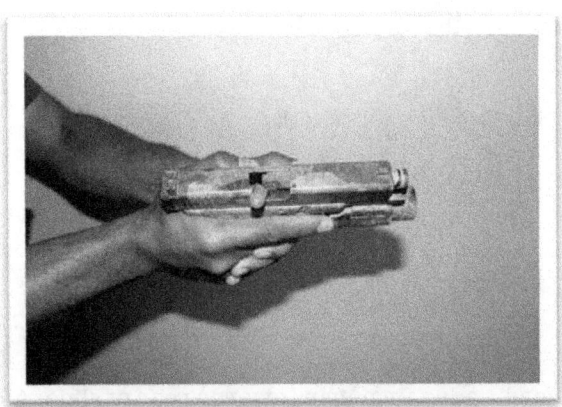

To Fix A Type 2 Malfunction Do The Following:

NOTE: Start by slightly canting firearm to allow for visual inspection of ejection port to identify stoppage. Also bring arms back allowing elbows to naturally rest on upper abdomen. This creates a natural working platform to work from allowing you to focus on your Threat while placing firearm in direct focal plane to allow you to still see your firearm utilizing peripheral vision.

NOTE: Firmly and generously tap the bottom of the magazine to assure it is properly seated.

NOTE: Obtain grip of your slide and sweep the stuck case free as you rack.

NOTE: ALWAYS obtain an over-handed firm grip towards rear of slide. Assure finger is outside trigger guard. Push forward with gun hand while pulling back with support hand to rack slide.

NOTE: Release grip of slide after pulling it all the way to the rear. Allow slide to slam forward on its own while also allowing support hand to naturally fling back towards chest. This assures your first round will properly load.

Type 3 Malfunction:

A Type 3 Malfunction is much more difficult to overcome and requires extra time. Meaning you'll have to move to cover, while mitigating this stoppage. This kind of malfunction almost exclusively occurs due to a faulty magazine. Basically the magazine spring losses it's springiness and fails to apply the required pressure that pushes rounds into your firearm's chamber. This is a VERY bad malfunction during a gunfight as it will take you out of the fight for a while. If you notice this type of malfunction while training, repair, discard or replace the magazine prior to carrying it for defensive use.

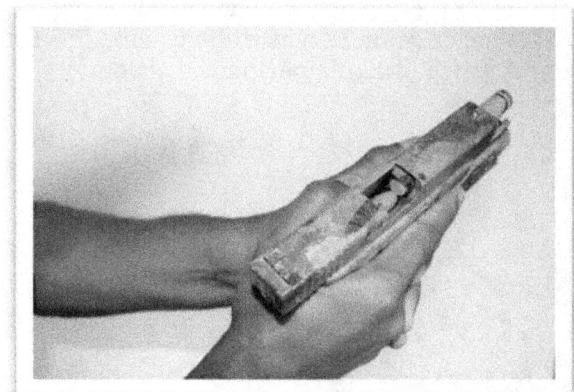 

To Fix A Type 3 Malfunction Do The Following:

NOTE: Start by slightly canting firearm to allow for visual inspection of ejection port to identify stoppage. Also bring arms back allowing elbows to naturally rest on upper abdomen. This creates a natural working platform to work from allowing you to focus on your Threat while placing firearm in direct focal plane to allow you to still see your firearm utilizing peripheral vision.

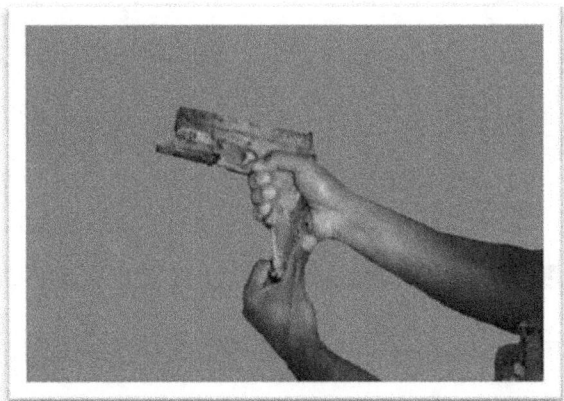

NOTE: Remove simulated partial magazine from firearm. This will be a difficult task since the first round is wedged in the chamber. You'll need to use diligent force.

NOTE: Now you'll need to violently rack your slide back and forth a few times to free the stuck round.

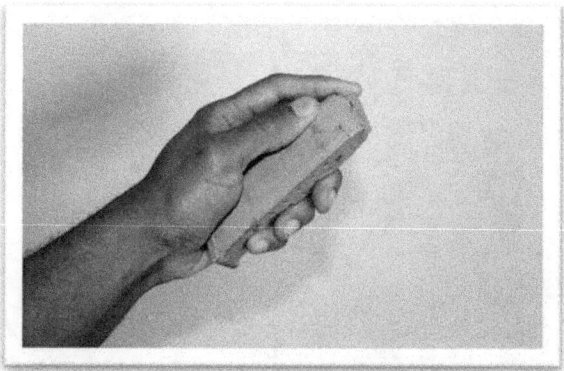

NOTE: Stage index finger on business end of Snap-Cap. This allows for more consistent loading while also assuring Snap-Cap is in correct position.

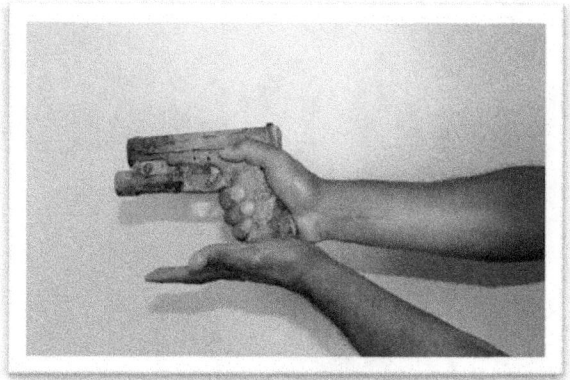

NOTE: Firmly and generously tap the bottom of the magazine to assure it is properly seated.

NOTE: Get into the habit of sweeping ejection port while obtaining grip of your slide when attempting to rack. This allows your brain to encode one solid movement for both Type 2 Malfunction clearing and normal racking.

NOTE: ALWAYS obtain an over-handed firm grip towards rear of slide. Assure finger is outside trigger guard. Push forward with gun hand while pulling back with support hand to rack slide.

NOTE: Release grip of slide after pulling it all the way to the rear. Allow slide to slam forward on its own while also allowing support hand to naturally fling back towards chest. This assures your first round will properly load.

Type 4 Malfunction:

A Type 4 Malfunction is the most difficult to overcome and should be considered a catastrophic mechanical failure of your firearm. This essentially renders your firearm completely inoperable, meaning you'll have to find another way to defend yourself. This kind of malfunction usually occurs due to a combination of faulty ammunition and or poor cleaning. The result is either a stuck casing in the breach or a lodged round in the barrel called a 'Squib Load'. Both outcomes require complete disassembly and tools to repair the stoppage. If you experience this type of malfunction during a gunfight, you have two choices. Either take the fight to the Threat physically or tactically re-deploy to cover.

Section 16
Basic Marksmanship

Your journey to becoming an efficient tactical marksman begins by first mastering the skills of a basic marksman. Marksmanship pertains to how well your body is able to marry itself to your weapon. Obtaining proficiency in the higher tempo arena of tactical marksmanship, means you've first learned the art of making your weapon an extension of yourself. That journey starts with mastering the following important techniques. The ZuluFight Dry-Fire Training System is key to this journey and will make the task of mastery an easier one.

1. Stance
2. Grip
3. Sight Alignment
4. Sight Picture
5. Breathing
6. Trigger Control
7. Follow Through
8. Trigger Reset

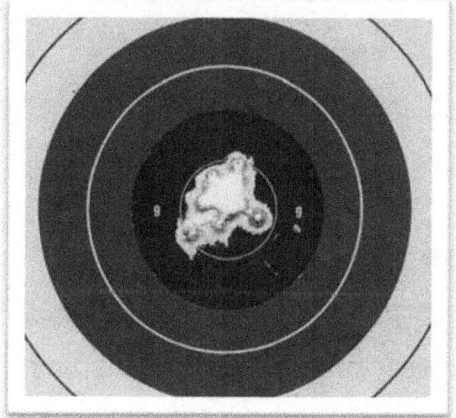

Stance:

Consistent and accurate shots down range begin with your base. Your base is what founds you to the ground it's what allows you to absorbed recoil. Without this base, your house comes troubling down. There are a number of different marksmanship stances available to you. The one that feels the most natural though is typically the best one for you.

Weaver Stance

The Weaver Stance is one of the more basic types of stance and the most common stance you'll find on shooting ranges. This stance is achieved by:

- Standing sideways from your target with your support shoulder facing your target.

- Your shooting arm crosses in front of your chest and is fully extended perpendicular to your support shoulder. This arm is used to absorb the forces of recoil and acts as the "Pushing" force of the stance.
- Your support arm is slightly bent with your elbow out to 9 O'clock. This arm provides the "Pulling" force of the stance.
- By Pushing with your strong arm and pulling back equally with your support, you create an extremely stable vise like grip.
- Easily acquired.
- Easily maintained for very extended periods of time
- The most accurate stance if only shooting "ONE" shot.
- Very difficult to accomplish tactical movement while also maintaining this type of stance.

Isosceles Stance

The Isosceles Stance derives its name from the shape of the shooter's arms. It is vastly different to the Weaver and most common amongst tactical shooters. This stance is achieved by:

- Squarely facing your target.
- Feet shoulder width apart.
- Slight bend at the knees with weight forward and over the balls of your feet.
- Arms locked straight forward forming the "Isosceles" triangle.
- Recoil is absorbed in both arms with the axis of recoil going in towards your chest.
- Easily acquired.
- Very easy to move while also maintaining a level shooting platform.
- Difficult to maintain for an extended period of time as it will cause your arms to eventually tier.

Natural Fighting Stance

This stance is the one which comes natural to you, and is the one you'll most certainly instinctively resort to upon attack. It's typically a slight modification of both the Weaver and the Isosceles and is similar to that of a basketball player's defensive stance. This type of stance is commonly referred to as the 'Modified Isosceles'. It should mirror the stance you resort to in a fight also known as your 'Tactical Stance'. Your dominant leg is typically the one that's slightly forward, with feet almost shoulder width apart. Your body is also in a slightly crouched or squatted position. This stance should offer you the following:

- STABILITY: Provides the proper balance left, right, backwards and forwards so as to absorb recoil, as well as punches, kicks or serious contact with your Threat during an up close and personal battle.

- MOBILITY: Provides the ability to naturally move left, right, backwards or forwards and at angles without trouble. Also provides ease of torso rotation at the waist, giving you the ability to track your Threat and shoot without moving your base.
- BALANCE: Balances both stability and mobility for an all-around fighting stance. To test this, acquire your stance then have someone push you from all angles to assure your base remains firm.

Tactical Fighting Stance

Natural Shooting Stance

Grip:

Your grip is a huge factor in your ability to absorb recoil and control the movement; or flip, of your firearm under recoil. This is especially true during multiple round engagements. When you depress the trigger and your firearm fires, it actually moves before the round exits the barrel. The more grip you apply as you fire will decrease the overall movement of your firearm in recoil, thereby allowing the bullet to fly straighter and flatter and much more accurately round to round.

The effects of recoil are very similar to that of water under hydraulic pressure. The pressure; or recoil, will follow the path of least resistance. Proper grip is accomplished by first obtaining a solid grip with your strong or shooting hand. Next your support hand fills the gaps left on the opposite side of the firearm's handle or grip with both thumbs resting against each other.

NOTE: Your first grip should be your last. Assure firearm is gripped high in web of thumb & trigger finger is staged outside trigger guard.

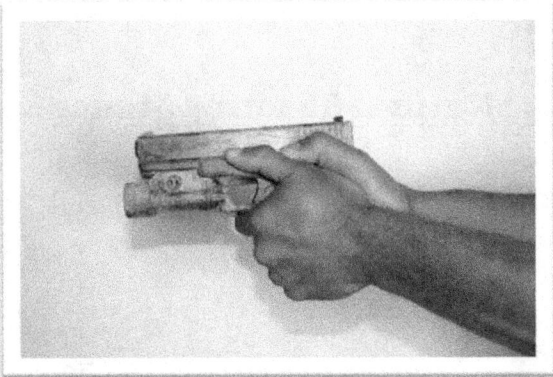

NOTE: The higher your grip is on your firearm, the closer it is to the axis of recoil. The closer your grip is to this point, the more egomaniacal your grip is, the easier it is to maintain and the better aligned your wrists, arms, shoulders and torso is to absorbing the recoil. This prevents the recoil from being directed over your arms which makes the firearm a lot snappier from round to round. 70% of grip should come from fingers of support hand. This allows for consistent & uninhibited trigger squeeze.

Sight Alignment:

Sight Alignment is achieved by equally aligning your front sight post with your rear sight notch. An easy way to remember this is 'Equal Height & Equal Light' Your front post is equal in height to your rear sight and there is equal light on each side of your front post. If your front sight post is positioned too far to the right, your bullet will strike right. If it's positioned too far up, your bullet will strike high.

Sight Picture:

Sight picture is the relationship between your perfectly aligned sights and your target or Threat. It's the action of overlaying your aligned sights and putting them where you wish to hit your Threat. For purposes of Basic Marksmanship, your front sight should be your focal point and in perfect focus, while your Threat should appear slightly blurred. In this case your bullet will strike just above your front sight post.

Breathing:

Proper oxygenation of your bloodstream is very important. Maintaining proper oxygenation levels will allow your muscles to work as they are supposed to. Holding your breath will cause your hands to trimmer and your eyes to lose focus. You should breath as normal as possible and when possible, shoot at the natural pause between breaths.

Trigger Control:

It's been said that 80% of accuracy deficiencies downrange is due to poor trigger control. Your trigger finger should 'Squeeze' the trigger, not pull or jerk it back. You should maintain consistent rearward pressure and speed all the way through the trigger squeeze. Typically, the best accuracy is achieved by using only the pad of your trigger finger. So avoid the urge of wrapping your whole finger around the trigger.

Follow Through:

Follow through is the concept of squeezing the trigger all the way rearward past the point at which the firearm discharges. Follow through is more of a cognitive thought than an action. It's a reminder to continue the 'Squeeze' past recoil. As the firearm flips back, you release the squeeze to Trigger Reset, allowing the firearm to fall back into alignment with your Threat.

Trigger Reset:

This is accomplished by slowly moving your trigger finger forward after Follow Through. Approximately halfway forward you will hear your trigger click and may even feel it. This is where your trigger resets and the position at which it is ready to be squeezed rearward again. Getting used to the position of your trigger's reset will greatly increase your overall accuracy due to the fact that it requires less overall movement.

Driving your Trigger:

When shooting multiple rounds, it's important to understand and become familiar with the 'Rhythm of Recoil', the pattern by which your firearm acts as it flips back and returns to rest and how that relates to trigger manipulation. This can be best understood by likening it to driving a car at high speeds around a tight corner. Too much gas; or jerky trigger pulling, and you'll spin out. Hit the brakes and you'll fishtail. Too much movement of the steering wheel and you'll lose control.

Mastering your firearm's Rhythm of Recoil is like mastering your car's RPM's. You must learn to input an appropriate amount of speed on the trigger, with just the right amount of grip combined with enough forward pressure and leaning on the firearm to allow your firearm the ability to fall back into alignment with your Threat for a level shooting platform for your next shot. Jerking the trigger will only cause you to shoot wildly, making accuracy a hopeless task.

Section 17
Situational Awareness
&
Threat ID

If you can't see your Threat, you can't beat your Threat. Threat Identification is an extremely important process and will greatly affect the outcome of your battle. Just as important as it is to identify your Threat, it's also important to know who's a Threat and who's not. When bullets start flying, the last thing you wanna do is turn around and blast granny by accident, when the guy who's shooting at you is actually standing next to her. This is why 'Situational Awareness' goes hand in hand with Threat Identification.

For the most part, your Threat is likely to be within arm's reach, however there are times when you could be attacked from across a room or even across a parking lot. There are also external factors such as low light, fog or even bright light, which could greatly diminish your ability to see your Threat. For these reasons it's vitally important that you develop the ability to correctly identify a Threat. It's also extremely important that you train your eyes to 'Seek'.

While this may sound straightforward, its actually not. If you lean back on your understanding from Chapter (2) of what happens physiologically during a fight, you'll realize just how difficult it is to differentiate things, while under attack, let alone to 'Seek' clarity and definition of the vastness of your environment. The best way to help train your eyes to 'Seek' is by incorporating ABC's Tactical Training Aides into your training sessions. To learn more about ABCs Tactical Awareness Aides, turn to Page 176.

DELTA Threat ID:

The most tactically effective Threat Identification technique was developed by the United States Special Forces. This five step process; when practiced, will assure you appropriately scan your environment the right way.

1. **Whole Body**: The first step is to cognitively thinking about 'Who' you're actually looking at. Is it a man or woman, adult or child? Who are they? Are they in a uniform? Do they have a badge? Could they actually be a friend? These are all very important questions one must train their minds to 'Think' while their eyes 'Seek'. Seeing a person's 'Whole Body' will help elevate the chances of you mistaking a friend for a foe.

2. **Hands:** Your next step is to find their 'Hands'. It's been said "It's the hands that kill." Finding someone's hands will aid in determining if the possible threat is armed or not. Are they armed with a weapon or holding a cell phone? Seeing a weapon does NOT mean to 'Shoot' or that they're a threat. They could actually be assisting you or a police officer. This is why all five steps are important.

3. **Waistband:** Now it's time to check their waistband. If you didn't see a weapon in their hand, it doesn't mean they're not hiding one on their waist or in their waistband. Visual check their waist. What are they wearing, could something be hidden there? These are questions you should be asking.

4. **Arm Span:** After this you need to check their immediate surroundings. Is there anything in there 'Reach' which could be used as a weapon? This will also give you the ability to identify other persons and or other potential hazards.

5. **Demeanor:** Lastly, you need to check their face and body language. This is the most overlooked step and usually be the key to uncovering the truth. Remember 90% of communication is 'Non-Verbal' meaning body language often times says all. You should be asking yourself if they appear happy, sad or even angry? Look into their eyes, are they letting off that they're hiding something or being tricky? Or does their demeanor tell you they're an innocent bystander or an armed citizen attempting to aid in your defense?

Each of these steps are extremely important in assuring that you correctly identify a Threat. Remember the most overlooked step is 'Demeanor'. You need to confirm that they actually 'Look' like a Threat, either through their facials or body language. Becoming proficient in this technique requires practice. It's most easily achieved during Stress Inoculation training like Force on Force Training simulations. However, an easy way start building solid Threat Identification habits, is by actively identifying random people on a daily basis. Follow the SOF Threat ID process as you interact with other people on a daily basis. Ask yourself if the random person approaching you is a 'Threat'? then follow the five easy steps. Doing this on a regular basis will cause your mind to develop a habit of always scanning your environment for possible threats and will keep you situationally aware at all times.

'Look' at what you're supposed to 'See':

The next area of importance is to 'Look' at what you're supposed to 'See'. What this means is, once you identify a Threat, focus on them. At that point nothing in the entire universe matters more that the person who's trying to kill you. It's vital that you can accurately read and track the Threat and determine their level of risk to your life. Looking at your gun-sights will <u>NOT</u> help you. Searching for your gun-sights will only distract you. Instead, track your Threat, identify their movements and begin the process of calculating their actions. This can only be achieved by maintaining optical clarity of your Threat. In a gunfight, Traditional Sight Alignment and Sight Picture are completely useless to you. Instead obtain a ZuluFight Sight Picture.

Traditional Sight Picture

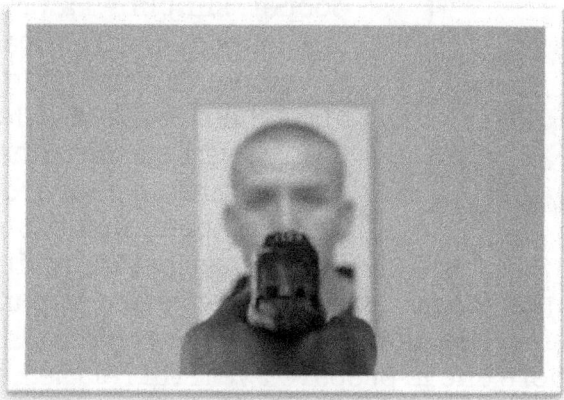

NOTE: Traditional Sight Picture. Sights in focus while threat is out of focus.

NOTE: ZuluFight Sight Picture. Threat is in focus while sights are out of focus.

The easiest way to understand this is to find a picture on a wall. Focus on a particular part of the image. Now point at the exact spot your looking and maintain visual clarity of the image, not your finger. Now cognitively identify your outstretched arm. You should barely notice your pointed finger which is blurry yet pointing at the exact spot you were looking. Aiming your gun at your threat in a gunfight is no different. Tell me something, do you look at your finger when you ring a door bell or do you focus on the door bell? It's the same thing. Present your firearm and ring your threat's door bell. You know that large thing protruding from the center of your Threat's face, just above his upper lip? That's his bell, so ring it!

Situational Awareness:

Maintaining a high level of 'Tactical Awareness' will assure that you are not just effective in identifying possible threats, but that you're also 'Aware' of your surroundings. Being aware of what's around you, will aid in your ability to locate places of cover, potential hazards, bystanders, backdrops or even arriving police officers. What it will also do is allow you to find your Threat's homeboys, who may be attempting to flank you during an attack.

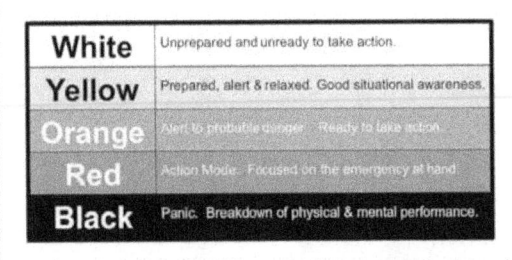

A tactical genius by the name of Col. Jeff Cooper, simplified a pretty practical approach to the concept of a Tactical Awareness by developing a color code of different mental awareness levels. He determined that to be ready for the randomness of an ambush, one must maintain a level of heightened neutrality. Meaning one must not be completely at rest. Otherwise that individual could be taken by 'Complete' surprise and upon attack, would easily revert to panic and would most certainly be doomed to defeat. He determined that by maintaining a balanced level of heightened neutrality, where one is prepared yet still relaxed, they could easily transition to a level of 'Alertness' and then 'Action' without reverting to complete panic and fear.

Being Situationally Aware, means your head is on a swivel and you're constantly scanning your environment. It means you're 'Seeking' to 'Identify' potential Threats both near and far. This is a skill that takes a ton of work for most people. For those of us fortunate to grow-up in the inner-city, we developed a high sense of awareness also called 'Street Smarts'. However, if you grew-up in the suburbs or out in the sticks, you'll likely struggle in this area. Don't lose hope, becoming proficient with this, can be done. It starts by actively scanning your environment at all times. That means when you walk out of a door, scan left then right just as you would when entering a roadway. When walking through the park, scan, look for potential Threats. Learn to use your peripheral vision and identify people who approach you. Train your peripheral awareness by determining if the person approaching or passing you is a Threat, without actually looking at them. Over time your overall level of Tactical Awareness will heighten and you'll develop the 'Habit' of being aware.

Section 18
Multi-Threat Engagement

Should you find yourself reacting to a deadly Threat, it's extremely likely you'll be faced with not one, but multiple Threats. Criminals are like wolves, they lurk in wait for helpless sheep and like wolves, they tend to travel in packs. This is why it's vitally important that you develop the habit of 'Situational Awareness'.

During a recent Active Shooter incident at a Las Vegas Walmart, an armed citizen learned this lesson the hard way. While sneaking-up on who he thought to be the 'Only' Active Shooter, the brave citizen ended-up getting flanked and gunned down by a second Active Shooter. While his actions were heroic, his death was most unfortunate and just may have been prevented had he assumed that there are ALWAYS multiple Threats.

As a Sniper, I learned to blend in and be sneaky. Over a period of time, I acquired an acute ability to become a Chameleon of sorts and operate undetected and unhampered in a variety of environments. This ability was founded on ONE principle. To remain unseen, you must first assume that someone is ALWAYS watching and that someone is an enemy Sniper who's about to shoot you in your face. This mindset means that every movement a Sniper makes, is taken with utmost care and is calculative by nature. It's as though you can literally feel the enemy Sniper's Mil-Dot Reticle resting on your face, causing your nose to itch.

In a similar way, you must ALWAYS assume there are multiple Threats at different angles, distances and behind EVERY blind spot. This degree of Tactical Awareness is assured to keep you in a state of readiness as you actively 'Seek' for Threats....plural.

Effective use of senses:

Identifying multiple Threats comes down to how well you use your senses. You must assure that you are reminding yourself to both 'Look' and 'Hear' the Threats who stalk you. As discussed previously, our bodies will experience a number of physiological effects when confronted with a deadly Threat. Due to the effects of Tunnel or Focused Vision, you will have a tendency to see only the Threat that's directly in front of you. Under extremely stressful situations like this, our ears are tethered to our eyes. Essentially they are hearing what our eyes are seeing.

The problem arises when you consider the likelihood of multiple Threats. If your eyes are laser focused on one individual, and due to the Laws of Combat, you've lost your peripheral vision, how in the world will you even see the other Threats?

The answer is by 'Resetting' your brain. Our brains are divided into multiple sections. For the most part though, we have a left and right side. Our sensory System is spider webbed throughout both sides of our brain. During times of extreme focus, it's important to 'Reset' allowing your brain the ability of regaining its Spatial Awareness. Similar to Situational Awareness, your Spatial Awareness allows you to understand the relation of thing to one another within your immediate vicinity. Your ability to regain a Spatial balance is essential if you're wanting to differentiate between one Threat and another.

This is best accomplished by actively 'Seeking' objects to your right and to your left sides, while also cognitively identifying particular objects to your right and to the left. Through cognitive seeking, your brain regains depth perception and in turn peripheral clarity. After your brain gains this vital data, it's internal GPS regains its signal. Essential your brain now knows where it is in relation to everything else.

If you're training for battle, its essential that you begin developing the habit of scanning your environment. Your brain is a muscle. The more you work a muscle, the fitter it becomes. By habitually keeping your head on a swivel, as you traverse the world around you, your brain develops an unconscious ability of being Situationally Aware. When it comes to Tactical Awareness, perfecting your 'After Action Scan' in training, helps your brain develop the unconscious ability to actively 'Seek' when your life is threatened. The more you perform this technique, the more ingrained it becomes.

The best way to perfect the After Action Scan, is to incorporate ABCs Tactical Awareness Aides in your training. They are specifically designed to cause your eyes to see and your brain to process, multiple different objects while also performing instantaneous calculations, to train your brain to quickly differentiate one thing from another. To learn more about how ABCs Tactical Awareness Aides can make you more aware, turn to Page 176.

After Action Scan

The After Action Scan is a cognitive based search and destroy technique. It's not a meaningless and lazy side-to-side movement of one's head. Too often you will see that fatal error being performed on many a firearms range, as they simply move their heads absent any though whatsoever. Shooters have either forgotten or failed to be properly educated on the purpose of this life saving technique. The purpose is to 'Seek' and 'Find' additional Threats to one's safety. It is also to 'Seek' and 'Find' locations of available cover. Falling into the habit of simply moving your head left and right, without cognitively seeking, will encode the movement without the thought, leaving you incapable of being able to maintain Tactical Awareness during a fight.

1st Check Left

NOTE: Check Left. After Action Scan is vital to maintaining effective situational awareness. During direct contact with your Treat, your body will naturally cause your vision to focus on your Threat which such a degree of clarity that everything else around you fades out of view. Encoding proper After Action Scans will allow your brain to literally recalibrate and allow for you to regain normal visual function.

2nd Check Right

NOTE: Now check right. Don't get lazy in training! Remember you're teaching yourself to ACTIVELY look or seek for something. You're not simply moving your head. Scan and SEEK out possible Threats and or positions of possible cover. Remember to look back at your Threat each time you scan from left to right.

3rd Check Left & Behind

NOTE: Now it's time to look behind you. Start by looking over your left shoulder. Remember to cognitively identify an object while doing so in training. This trains your brain to instinctively SEEK as opposed to blindly gaze.

4th Check Right & Behind

NOTE: Now it's time to look over your right shoulder. As you transition right, be sure to identify your Threat to assure they're no-longer a threat. As you look over your right shoulder you should also cognitively identify an object behind you. Our ingenious ABCs Tactical Awareness Aides are the best way to perfect your After Action Scans. They're inexpensive and extremely easy to use. Use them each time you train.

Engaging Multiple Threat:

Our bodies are designed in a way that we can only do <u>ONE</u> thing effectively at any given time. Forget about Hollywood action movies, where you see someone running from one place to another, engaging a mass of enemy fighters, all while blazing away with two guns. Arming yourself with two guns only makes you twice as useless. The answerer to defeating multiple Threats comes down to strategy. While your enemies play Checkers, you're going to play Tactical Chess. This is accomplished in two ways:

1. **Spreading the Love:** If you have multiple Threats actively engaging you, it means you need to actively engage them as simultaneously as possible. Shoot them all, equally. The more time you spend engaging one particular Threat, means your other Threat(s) have more time to engage you.

    - One way to Spread the Love, is to shoot in a pattern. If you have (2) Threats, you would shoot each Threat once or twice, then quickly transition and shoot the other once or twice.

    - Another way is to randomly engage each Threat. Maybe you have (3) Threats and you choose to shoot your closest Threat three times, your next Threat twice and your last Threat once. Then you shoot your closest Threat once, move next Threat and shoot them twice and end by shooting your last Threat in the head.

2. **Movement:** By moving you make yourself a much harder target to kill. Also through the action of movement, you begin the process of causing your Threats to react to you.

    - One way is to use a blocking technique. This is accomplished by moving at angles so as to place objects, blind spots or even your Threat's accomplices, between you and your closest Threat. The idea is to eliminate a particular Threat's ability to continue engaging you, because they either can't see you or you've placed an object between them making it harder to engage you.

    - Another technique is to increase distance between you and your Threats. By increasing the distance, you decrease the amount of hip rotation and torso movement required to "Spread The Love." This is because as you move back and away from your Threats, you gain an ever increasing view of them. Pretty soon they will all be in front of you, making them much easier engage.

    - Flanking your Threats is another example of this. As opposed to moving backwards, you simply rush to the far right or left side of one of your Threats. At some point during this movement you will essentially have all of your Threat's lined up like ducks in a row. You will also create a situation where your farthest Threats have to shoot through or past their buddies in order to engage you. That's what's called a 'Force Multiplier' in the tactical world.

However, you choose to engage multiple Threats, you need to do so dynamically, with speed and with violence of action. You need to turn the tables as quickly as possible, and cause your Threats to react to you. The wolves who seek your blood may have trained to coordinate their attacks; it is however very unlikely they've trained in coordinating a response to your attack. Turn the tide, be quick and be deadly.

Section 19
Defensive Shooting

The Laws of Combat and their effect on the human body, creates a substantial conundrum of sorts, when it relates to marksmanship. Hits count! On the range it can mean the difference between a pat on the back or a trophy at your next 3 Gun match. In a fight for your life though, a miss could mean you don't go back to your family. The problem is that most shooters build their entire defensive shooting posture, on sand. When the Apocalyptic Tsunami of Combat comes, its affect washes away one's ability to remain accurate.  This is precisely why police officers have a pitiful 20% hit ratio in real-world shootouts. Their attackers have a 90% hit ration. Why, because when you're under attack, your 'Reacting' to a completely unknown Threat to your existence.

The concept of 'Marksmanship' is not easily translated in a tactical environment. With that being said, there is a huge difference between 'Range Marksmanship' and 'Tactical Marksmanship'.

Marksmanship on the range is accomplished by mastering eight important elements. The level of one's expertise, is depended upon their ability to effectively balance all eight components, in a harmonious orchestra of kinesis.

1. Stance

2. Grip

3. Sight Alignment

4. Sight Picture

5. Breathing

6. Trigger Control

7. Follow Through

8. Trigger Reset

On the Range; where there is a complete absence of Combat Stress, these (8) components to accuracy, are the ingredients to a bull's-eye. On the range you have the ability to think through, slowdown and control each movement independently. However, in a gunfight your ability to control your movements, is greatly diminished. In a gunfight, you're frantically reacting to a lethal Threat, you're not shooting bulls-eyes. As discussed previously, the Laws of Combat and their overall effect on your physiology to a great extent, prevent you from achieving the (2) most important elements of 'Range Marksmanship' while also greatly diminishing (4) others. This means in a gunfight your left with the possibility of only being effective in but (2) areas of Marksmanship.

A Two Legged Stool:

Have you ever attempted to sit on a two legged stool? It can be done, but it requires a constant awareness of balance and an absence of distraction. What do you think the overall affect (10) shots of rum would have, on your ability to control your balance, while attempting to sit on a stool with only two legs? The intoxicating effects from the cocktail of Combat is unmatched. If you rely on Range Marksmanship in a gunfight, you're gonna miss 80% of the time. Here's why:

1. **Non-existent Sights:** Sight use is the cornerstone to effective marksmanship at the range. Force Science has proven that it is virtually impossible to even see your gun-sights in a gunfight. The physiology of a gunfight, means the only thing you'll see; with clarity, is the person(s) trying to kill you. This all important Law of Combat, is as catastrophic as a nuclear meltdown if your gun-fighting skills have been built on the tenets of Traditional Sight Use, or Sight Alignment and Sight Picture.

2. **Soup Sandwich:** The very same Laws of Combat greatly hamper our ability to perform (4) more all important elements to success on the range.

    - Your ability to control breathing is non-existent. You will breath but it will be fast and it will be random. The idea of shooting at the end of your exhale in close Combat, is impossible.

    - Trigger manipulation is also diminished. This represents (3) equally important functions:
        - Trigger Control
        - Follow-Through
        - Trigger Reset.

The reality is that in combat; unless you've undergone Procedural Memory training; like ZuluFight, you're going to slap, yank and jerk your trigger. What you're left with is a Soup Sandwich that tastes a lot like the stuff that comes out of a cow's ass. Losing your ability to hit your Threat, while they effortlessly put holes in you, is a pitifully bitter pill to swallow.

Combat Hydraulics:

As discussed previously, Combat is the most chaotically charged, out of control, consistently dynamic environment one will ever find themselves. It's measured in splits of seconds and its force is greater than the convergence of entire oceans. The only way to assure you react with a Tactical Squared Response, is by preparing for that battled beforehand. This is accomplished in (3) ways:

3. **Training The Psyche:** The first ingredient to s Tactical Squared Response is by preparing your mind for the psychology of Combat. It's vital that you devour and understand the science of Combat itself. You must learn about its effects and how you can counter or better manage them. Having a firm grasp on this all-important truth, will prevent you from experiencing 'Combat Paralysis' or Condition Black as Col. Cooper put it. Knowing what WILL happen physiologically, will greatly decrease the psychological effects. Preparing today, will assuring you choose a training method, which will actually translate to a 'Win' tomorrow.

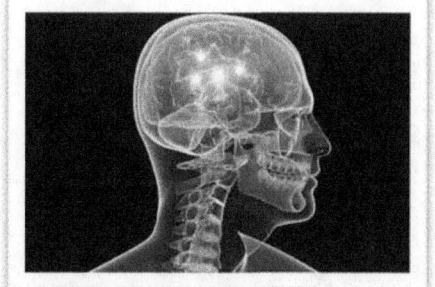

4. **Training The Body:** The next step is to adopt and commit yourself to a practical training system capable of encoding the appropriate Fight Responses, for tomorrow's battle. Sun Tzu tells us that a skilled warrior fights his battle a thousand times before he's even met his enemy. Training your body; by developing the habits of success, is a vital ingredient to success in Combat. The ZuluFight Dry-Fire Training System is the easiest way at achieve this. There is no better way to prepare one's body for war and to master the Kata of Firearms Self-Defense, than through Procedural Memory Encoding. It's how the Samurai of old became so deadly and its exactly how the members of our Special Operations Community train for battle. Mastering the kinesis of battle, requires a copious amount of repetition over an extended period of time. There's no better way to do this than through Dry-Fire Training. ZuluFight takes Dry-Fire to a whole new level of mastery. It's how you'll develop practical, effective and deadly instinctive solutions for tomorrow's battle. Turn to Page 173 to learn more.

5. **Playing Tactical Chess:** The last ingredient to a Tactical Squared Response is the development of effective Fighting Tactics. In a gunfight, your voodoo needs to be better than your Threat's. What you do in response to their attack, WILL determine all. We all know that book-smart geek; the know-it-all, who couldn't find their way out of a Cracker Jacks box. Simply being book-smart and knowing the science behind Combat, is useless if you neglect to develop actual Fighting Skills based on that knowledge. Skills without strategy are meaningless in Combat. We've all likely met the guy who knows how to shoot a basketball and consistently make half-court shots, yet hasn't a clue on how to actually 'Play' a real game. The concept of 'Tactical Chess' is where you infuse proven, practical and effective Fighting Tactics into your Tactical Response. Movement, repetitive fire, cover and blocking techniques, these are all ingredients; that when melded together and directed in a controlled manner, afford you the ability to place your Threat in checkmate and win the day. An easy

and effective way to learn practical and proven battle techniques, is by attending tactical shooting classes. Seek out training classes that teach dynamic movement and Force-on-Force simulation. Zulu Tactical provides a number of tactical courses, focused on providing its students with tactical solutions that actually work. Seeking out competent instruction is how you turn knowledge into Combat effective action.

Tactical Shooting Positions:

Being able to shoot on the move and from a myriad of different positions, is a key ingredient to winning a gunfight. A true tactical shooting position means that once acquired, the shooter can effectively engage their Threat(s) accurately and constantly, without having to constantly change their base. The following are a few practical shooting positions which should be practiced and encoded:

Tactical Stance

NOTE: Your Tactical Stance is a vital ingredient to your overall fighting solution. The best most practical position should consist of a staggered stance with a comfortable bend in your knees. You should easily be able to move in any direction while also being able to absorb physical contact from any direction. This position should NOT change during the draw or while shooting and is the basis for a Modified Isosceles Stance.

Natural Shooting Stance

NOTE: Bring sights up and level to eyes not eyes to sights. Feet should be staggered with comfortable bend in knees. The Modified Isosceles Stance is hands down the BEST tactical stance. It allows for the best overall mobility. Notice firearms is level with eyes and focus is on threat NOT sights.

C. Q. B. Ready

NOTE: This position is a perfect shooting platform at close quarters but is also the natural position to obtain a two-handed grip. Your elbows are brought tight against your sides and your firearm placed directly in front of you and level. From this position your torso becomes a turret mounted gun. You aim by simply squaring your shoulders towards your Threat. The key to maintaining a level firearm from this position is to lock your wrists and positioning your elbows against your sides as opposed to resting them on your stomach.

SUL Ready

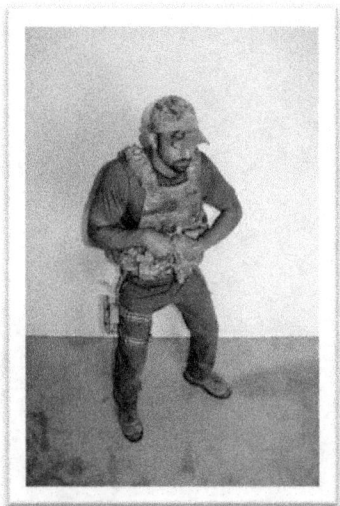

NOTE: SUL is Portuguese for 'South' the direction of the muzzle. Obtaining this grip is easily performed by indexing both thumbs together remembering the firearm always rests on top of your support hand. SUL is the most practical handgun carry position as it provides the safest muzzle disciple while also allowing for ease of draw. SUL is also the safest handgun carry position while moving and or maneuvering around obstacles. Drawing from SUL is easy. Simply pivot your thumbs while lifting and pushing your handgun up and out. As you extend your arms, allow your support hand to naturally pivot into your two-handed grip.

Close Ready

NOTE: Close Ready is intended for firing from contact distance or within two feet. Simply lock your gun arm tight against your side with an OVERGRIP of the handgun. Accurate shot placement is similar to C.Q.B. Ready. Utilize your torso and squared shoulders as a sort of turret aiming device. It's important to raise your support hand in front of you. It's inevitable that at this distance you will make physical contact with the Threat. Having your support arm positioned in this manner will help provide a solid defensive posture while also giving you the ability to maintain safe distance so your firearm can properly function and reload. Making contact on your Threat with the muzzle while shooting will turn your semi-auto handgun into a single-shot paperweight.

Warrior Mentality:

There is a difference between a 'Warrior' and a 'Fighter'. Above all else, your greatest chance of surviving a deadly encounter, rests on your internal obsession to 'Win' no matter the cost.

A Fighter, fights from a mindset rooted in competition. His goal is to beat his adversary by points and averages, while also accepting the belief that if his opponent is better, than a 'Lose' is probable. When it gets tough, when the sting of battle overwhelms him, the Fighter will concede for fear of injury.

To the contrary, the Warrior, fights with the mindset of a ruthless killer. To a certain degree, he's acquired a particular kind of bloodlust. He forgoes attempts of trying to avoid the unavoidable pain that's coming because he knows pain will come. Instead, his strategy is based on his expectation and acceptance of the sting of battle. He welcomes it with open arms because he has prepared for it ahead of time. He's developed a certain inoculation to pain and is ready to absorb its bite. He knows he will be shot, he will lose blood, he will experience injury, he will be caught off-guard, he will have to fight an uphill battle against all odds and that nothing will be fare. Yet he has already determined to kill his enemy, win the battle and return home.

While the Fighter fights to counter and avoid the inevitable, the Warrior has prepared and developed a solution capable of overcoming those odds, even under the worst conditions. Combat is not a competition, but basketball is and so are IPSC and 3 Gun matches. Combat is not a game; 'Call of Duty' is a game. Pin Pong, tennis, baseball, Risk.....These are competitions. Wrestling, MMA and UFC... these are extreme forms of competition. In a competition there are rules, parameters and limits. Both parties walk away to fight another day. In Combat there are no rules, no boundaries and no restraint. There are no second place Combat ribbons; those have been replaced with an obituary and a flag draped coffin. Failure in competition results in a loose, with a chance to meet again. Failure in Combat results in death, for which there is no coming back.

A competitor 'Stops' his opponent by countering their movements, thereby halting momentum. At some point their opponent concedes due to exhaustion or fear of injury. A Warrior on the other hand, stuns his enemy. He digs to his depths and retrieves the most instinctively vicious, most barbarically unrelenting and unimaginable carnage. His response completely surprises his Threat and sends shivers up their spine. The Warrior's fight is a brutally heinous, focused energy that jolts his antagonist at their core. It saps them of their willingness to proceed. At some point a Warrior's enemy actually believes they're looking into the eyes of a demonic being. That is the mentality of Warrior and the mindset you must acquire. You must devourer your enemy like a crazed lion.

FBI Miami Shootout April 11th 1986

- The gunfight lasted just over 4-minutes.
- Both suspects were shot within the first 30-seconds.
- The first suspect; Matix, sustained multiple gunshot wounds and injured multiple officers. Matix continued to fight for over 3-minutes before finally dying.
- The second suspect, Platt's first wound was the fatal shot. His first wound was from a 9mm through his right shoulder. It entered his chest, collapsed a lung and penetrated his heart.
- Platt continued to fight and killed with ease for 3 ½ more minutes.
- Platt advanced on Agents killing two and severely injuring five more Agents.
- Platt sustained eleven more wounds while advancing on Agents. Eight of those wounds were to the chest.

- Platt used three firearms. His own, Matix's and even executed his own killer with that Agent's own weapon before, dying 2 ½ minutes later. How's that for irony?
- Platt's cause of death was his first wound. By the end of the shooting he had 1 ½ liters of blood in his longs and died by drowning.
- When interviewed, the final Agent left standing informed investigators that there was a turning-point in the battle, where that Agent made the conscious decision to actually 'Kill' Platt not just 'Stop' him. He expressed that it wasn't until he determined to 'Kill' his attacker, that the tides changed.

Florida Highway Shooting

- A suspect attempts to disarm a trooper during a traffic stop.
- Trooper shoots the suspect once in the upper abdomen with a contact shot from his 1911 45 ACP service pistol, but chooses not to keep shooting.
- Suspect retrieves his concealed Derringer .22 caliber. Then shoots and kills the trooper with one shot in the trooper's armpit.

Utah Mall Active Shooter

- Shootout occurred at a distance of 4-feet, between SWAT and the suspect.
- SWAT shot the suspect with nine fatal shots in the chest from full-auto MP5s. The suspect's heart exploded as the result of the first two of these rounds.
- The suspect continued to fight and shot at the SWAT Operators with a shotgun, barely missing one of the Operator's heads.
- The suspect was finally killed with six more full-auto shots to his head.

Oregon Suicidal Subject

- A suicidal female advances on 2 Deputies from 60-meters, while shooting at them with her Glock 17.
- The Deputies' 1st shot was fatal. He literally blew the suspect's heart open with a 1oz shotgun slug.
- Suspect continued to advance while shooting without staggering.
- Suspect closes to within 20-yards sustaining three more wounds.
- Suspect collapsed to the ground due to blood lose, but was still able to fire at the Deputies.
- Suspect turned the gun on herself, shot herself three times in the chest and two times in the face.
- Cause of death was ruled to be the final shot to the face.
- Another example that just because you inflict a 'Fatal' shot to your Threat, even if it blows their heart open, it doesn't mean the fight is over. You have to 'Kill' them before they die.

These are but a few examples of what actually occurs in gunfights. Sadly, the list could go on and on. None of these individuals were intoxicated or high on drugs at the time of the incidents. All of them were determined to kill the good guys. All of them sustained devastating and fatal wounds at the onset of the battle. All of them continued to fight regardless of their wounds. Just because your Threat's heart is blow apart, it does NOT mean you won. Science says they could still fight for up to four more minutes.

In a real gunfight, victory goes to he who's more determined to 'Kill'. Platt is a perfect example of this. Agent Ben Gorgan blew Platt's heart open with his first round. Yet Platt was more determined. Platt became the hunter. Platt advanced while laying down fire with his Mini-14, pinning down Agent Gorgan. Platt was hit numerous times during that advance, yet he still tracked Agent Gorgan down and shot him execution style. At that point in the battle, it was eight to one with the odds stacked against Platt. Platt took six of them out of the fight single handed.

The FBI's excuse for such an unbelievable ass kicking was ammunition. For the last 30-years the FBI has staunchly blamed their failure that day on the 9mm Luger, claiming it to be an inferior round in battle. They went as far as to develop the 40 S&W, which has proved to be a pathetically poor substitute. Finally, after all this time they have accepted the truth and have returned to the 9mm Luger as their go to round. Why, because they knew all along that their failure that day was because they failed to properly train their Agents for war.

It wasn't the rounds fired which proved to be ineffective, it was the inferiority of the Agents' fight. It was a defeated mindset which was founded on inaccurate assumptions of Combat, that caused Agents to accept defeat itself. It was their inferior training, which lacked the strategy. It was the Agent's inability to employ solid Team Tactics, so as to coordinate their response, which caused them to be pinned down and overrun. The suspects however, had the mindsets of ravage lions. They knew what to expect before they got there. Most notably, they were NOT going to stop killing until their bodies were drained of its blood. They acceded pain and welcomed its sting. They knew what mattered most was the speed, the veracity and the violence of their action. They knew the faster they were able to inflict multiple hits on their pursuers, the quicker they'd fall. They were trained to take the fight to the enemy and 'Kill' with vengeance.

Your survival in a gunfight is completely depended upon your will to 'Kill' your Threat, before they kill you. Your ability to kill your Threat is completely depended upon your degree of preparation. Your preparation is measured by your knowledge of the dynamics of Combat, your aptitude with your weapon and your overall ability to turn the tide of the battle, through the application of solid fighting tactics.

It's about the 'Violence of Action' not mere action. When you violently send rapidly expanding rounds into multiple different areas of your Threat's body, it initiates total body meltdown. As those rounds impact, electric currents are sent through their

Central Nervous System like ripples on calm water. However, by sending multiple rounds in close succession, those ripples intersect, thereby scrambling the pattern and completely disrupting their brains ability to decipher what's happing. Meltdown begins, their blood becomes thin and unable to clot. Their blood pressure and heart rate skyrockets, bringing about a catastrophic failure as their blood pours from wound to wound.

When you face your Threat you must NOT mistake that he is trying to kill you. Unless you kill them first, he WILL achieve his objective. There are no do-overs, no time-outs and no re-spawning. In Combat, defeat is fatal and it is final. It's up to you to determine today that you will win, no matter the cost.

Section 20
Zulu's Top Picks

You've decided to arm yourself to hedge against an attack on your existence. You don't know when or where this attack may occur, but you've decided to be ready. Do you have the 'Best' tool for the job? Is there even a such thing as the best firearm, or does it come down to personal preference?

I'm going to argue that there is a best choice for Personal Defense. There is a plethora of choices out there, many are completely impractical, while some are okay and a few are decent and should get the job done. However, there are a specific breed of handgun, which are inherently better suited for Personal Defense, no matter the circumstance or environment. This chapter is focused on giving you my Top 3 Full-Size, Concealed Carry and Sub-Compact handguns as well as the best caliber and ammunition choices.

The right choice...

There are thousands of different types of handguns from hundreds of different manufactures, but not all handguns are created equal. When determining the right handgun for Personal Defense, there are a few key factors to keep in mind:

1. **Suited:** The reason you're even acquiring a weapon is to 'Defend Life'. It's NOT for looks, plinking at the range or for competition. It's for the sole purpose of Self-Defense. What it boils down to, is you require a Combat Handgun. You need something specifically suited for gunfights not a show gun. The handgun itself must by nature be:

    - Practical
    - Reliable
    - Simplistic

It's important your handgun's inherent qualities are practical and afford ease of use under varying circumstances. For instance, one overlooked reality of Firearms Self-Defense, relates to the fluidity of movement during the fight. The veracity of this movement has a direct effect on the functionality of any given handgun. One of the most common handgun failures is the Type 2 Malfunction and pertains 'Yaw Effect. This is where the handgun is exposed to twisting or an oscillation of movement off its vertical axis, while in the process of shooting or recoil. Basically gravity acts against recoil and the firearm fails to fully eject its spent casing. If there's one thing you can be certain of, it's that your fight WILL be dynamic and be subject to continual movement with a constantly changing shooting platform. So when it comes to practicality you'll want to make sure you choose a handgun that will perform well despite the veracity by which you fight.

Good Ol Murphy loves to pop his head up when we can least afford it. You can bet he'll be there during your fight. For this reason, it's critical that you choose the most reliable option out there. You need a handgun that will work no matter what, regardless of the abuse. While all Combat Handguns are suited for a fight, some are far more dependable for ANY fight regardless of when and where. You'll need to realize that you'll likely be carrying your handgun on a daily basis. Because of this your gun will be exposed to things like, lint and dust, as well as many other substances. Your handgun will also experience the extreme changes of temperature and humidity as you regularly go from the comfortable conditions of your home, car or office, to the extremes of the outdoors. All of these factors directly affect your handgun's functionality. Some Handguns require far more maintenance than others, simply to keep them functional. Some handguns are specifically designed to function even under the worst conditions, without regular maintenance. You need a Timex, a handgun that takes a lickin but keeps on tickin.

The most frustratingly consistent reality about almost every incident of Self-Defense, relates to the fact that 'Action' is always faster than 'Reaction', and you're almost always 'Reacting' to a deadly threat. Time is NOT on your side. In Chapter (2) we learned that when reacting to a shooting Threat, you could easily be shot 6-10 times before you're even capable of shooting back. Is there any sense in adding more reaction time by choosing to fight with a weapon that's harder to use and requires multiple manipulations, just to get it to shoot? Simplicity is key! Your handgun's functionality should adhere to the Keep It Simple Stupid (KISS) methodology. It should be streamlined, free from unneeded accessories, capable of ambidextrous shooting and more of a 'Point and Shoot' gun as opposed to one that requires the manipulation of safeties and other buttons. When the shit hits the fan and your life is determined by the speed and violence of your fight, you're NOT gonna want a $600-$700, 3lb paperweight that you can't get off 'Safe'. KISS, it works every time.

1. **Tailored:** All Combat Handguns are suited for the task of fighting and all will get the job done, however which one is 'Best' for you comes down to your mission. If you knew the time and place of attack, then you'd bring a rifle and about 10 friends with rifles, but you don't and you can't. So your objectives for Personal Defense pertain mainly to proactive daily preparation or Concealed Carry / Home Defense. There are (3) types of Combat Handguns:

    - Full-Size
    - Compact / Concealed Carry
    - Sub-Compact / Pocket Carry

It's best to select a handgun that's suited for the particular task at hand. If you're defending your home, a Full-Size handgun is 'Best' suited. So tailoring your Home Defense gun to a Full-Size variant would be best. If it Summer time and you've decided to head out on the town, a Full-Size gun would probably be completely impractical, since you'll likely be wearing shorts and a t-shirt. So in this case, you may need to resort to a Sub-Compact variant. Even though the Sub-Compact variant is say 'Three Stars' to the Full-Size's 'Five Stars', your mission dictates your equipment, so choose the best Sub-Compact option available. Your mid-sized or compact options are a great alternative because they offer the best of both worlds. There may even be occasions when you'll need an extremely small gun, which fits in your pocket. Whatever your choice is just remember to tailor the handgun to your mission and purchase a handgun that scores high in Practicality, Reliability and Simplicity.

Which gun is best?

This is by far the biggest controversy amongst firearms owners in forever. I'll admit there might not be a Holy Grail of Combat Handguns, but most handguns are not a viable option for an actual gunfight. They're just not suited for the task. Since your fight will ultimately be based on you attempting to protect your life, wouldn't it be wise to show up to that fight with the very best weapon capable of helping you win that fight? However, if you're not a tactical professional, how do you go about finding out which handguns to avoid? You accomplish this by learning what's most important in a gunfight. You weed-out the guns that won't work by prioritizing what's most important in a gunfight. Which is, multiple rounds on Threat, in the shortest of time spans, regardless of the circumstances, all the time, every time. I'm going to show you my Top 3 picks but it's up to you to decide what makes the most sense.

We just discussed the importance of going with a weapon that's both Suits and is Tailored to the fight. As we discussed, a Combat or Tactical Handgun, is specifically designed for a gunfight. Most Combat Handguns will get the job done, however there is one that stands out as the most practical, dependable and reliable handgun for tactical purposes. It's also one hated by many. Why, because most people simply don't understand Combat itself or the power of 'Simplicity' as a defense. The more complicated something is, the more likely it is to fail, especially under stress. As you've learning in Chapter (2), there's no place more stress ridden than the middle of a fight for your life.

Since the Flintlock, the Revolver style handgun is 1st Generation handgun technology. There is a reason why the Revolver was replaced in battle. While they are compact and pretty easy to use, they do not provide the tactical advancements of a decent semi-auto. Hence they are NOT suited for a fight. Due to a complete lack of fighting experience by the vast majority of firearms enthusiasts, the Revolver is still the go to Concealed Carry firearm for many an armed citizen.

One of the main proponents to why people inadvertently show-up to a gunfight with inferior weapons, goes all the way back to the purchase of those weapons. Unfortunately, many gun store clerks push the Revolver because of their simplicity. However, simplicity itself is NOT the only factor which makes-up a solid Combat Handgun. Revolver have three huge setbacks. They simply don't hold enough rounds, are horribly difficult to reload under pressure and lack the ergonomics of modern day handguns. Gun dealers ignore these truths. Instead they believe new shooters; especially ladies, don't have the ability to carry semi-autos. What's crazy is that if given a choice between the two, that same clerk would take a semi-auto over even the most well-made Revolver. Remember, your whole reason for owning a handgun, is because you believe that someday you'll need to use it to protect your life or someone else's. You need to show-up to that fight with the best tool suited and tailored for that fight.

In the 1890's a tactical genius by the name of John M. Browning, took it upon himself to devise a more practical Combat Handgun to replace Samuel Colt's 1830's Revolver. The Revolver was outdated and had become a hindrance in battle. What was needed was a more ergonomically correct, semi-automatic, which could be more easily reloaded on the move and could hold more rounds. They also needed a weapon which was capable of withstanding the abuse of battle as well as its exposure to sand, dirt and weather. Browning's new design literally changed the face of battle and has proved to be just as revolutionary as his machine gun advancements.

In fact, the M1911 Pistol went on to be the longest serving firearm in American History. For 100 years its stood as the Gold Standard of modern Combat Handguns. Like a number of tried and tested weapons of its era, the 1911 Pistol is still as lethal today as it was in the 1890's. However, like anything, times change and so does technology.

Think about the aerospace industry and its role in modern warfare. In the very same year that the 1911 Pistol was introduced to the battlefield, so to was the single-seat prop engine 1911 Deperdussin Monoplane. Most people wouldn't even know it, but if it hadn't been for this now archaic monoplane, we wouldn't have the F-22 Raptor, F-16 Fighting Falcon or any of our modern attack fighters. Could you imagine though, showing up to a Dog Fight next week flying a Monoplane?

The 1911 Pistol is a fine weapon but its old 2nd Generation technology, going on 126 years and counting. In that span of time, things have changed and weaponry has evolved into a much more efficient and practical design.

In 1982 another tactical genius Austrian born; Gaston Glock, took the semi-auto pistol to a whole new world. Since then, the Glock 17 went Platinum and has set a whole new standard in modern day weaponry. The Glock is by far the most straight forward Combat Handgun in existence. It's also the easiest semi-auto handgun to operate by novice and experts, men and women, big or small. It's truly the closet thing you'll get to a 'Point and Shoot' weapon.

It's specifically designed to adhere to the KISS methodology and is probably the main reason many of its decenters have issue with it. Most notably the Glock does not have a dedicated safety. Why, because the only safety a Combat Handgun should have, is the acuitive judgment of the person who's employing the weapon itself. If you think back to the torrent of outside stressors that you'll face when you're attacked and the realities of Action vs. Reaction discussed in Chapter (2), you'll quickly understand why taking extra time to manipulate a safety, would NOT be ideal during a gunfight.

Some would argue that with practice, it takes no time at all to teach one's self to manipulate a safety during a gunfight. I would argue wholeheartedly against that. I've been in numerous incidents where very well trained individuals have forgotten to disengage their safeties in a fight and been left pulling on a trigger that even the Hulk couldn't make work. Ask around and you'll find this to be a very common and deadly reality. The reason is that when those individuals saw a Threat to their existence and their minds conceived a way to fight that Threat, the only thing their fingers remembered was to depress the trigger. Due to the stress, they forgot about the safety. Yet let's say you are able to disengage the safety, it will still take around a quarter second. Again if you remember about Reaction Times in Chapter (2), you'll know that in that quarter second, the Treat could easily send (1) round your direct. What if that round hits you in your face? That doesn't sound offal 'Safe' to me. Even if your Threat misses, how much time do really wanna waste fumbling around pushing buttons or flipping switches? The reality is that in a gunfight, when you're acting in Self-Defense, time is NOT on your side and you'll want a weapon that's simple and effective.

Others would argue that a Glock is not as accurate as say a Wilson Combat 1911. Well that may be true, but the variance of accuracy between an out of the box $450 Glock, compared to a $5,000 Wilson, only amounts to about quarter inch at best. When it comes to handgun battles and handgun distances, that quarter inch is meaningless, especially when you take into account the practical advantages the Glock affords over the 1911.

A Glock is far more agronomical for nearly everyone, making it both easier to manipulate and shoot. It's also much lighter than a 1911. This too is an area of argument, because some refer to the Glock as a 'Plastic Gun'. However, if I can drive a dump truck over my Glock, retrieve it, depress the trigger and know without a shadow of a doubt, that it will operate flawlessly, then I'm not so worried about it's so called 'Plastic' frame. In fact, the Polymer 2 frame is scientifically more resilient than carbon steel and most other steel alloy guns, to include the 1911. That's scientific fact. Think about it, Polymer 2 is what you call a 'Technology Advancement' kinda like Titanium is to the aerospace industry. Polymer 2 costs less to produce, meaning you pay less and it weighs less than a steel framed gun. That's a win in my book all day long. The Glock also has far fewer parts than all of its competition. Less parts means an exponential decrease in potential malfunctions, making it an inherently more dependable system altogether. Another advantage to a less moving parts, means the Glock is extremely easy to clean and maintain.

Glocks also boast of Double Stack Magazines, while 1911's only has Single Stacks. It's always better to have more and not need than to need it and not have enough. A Glock 17 affords you (18) ways to kill your Threat, while a standard 1911 only gives you (8). On top of all this, the Glock is the Timex that takes a lickin and keeps on tickin. You can abuse the Glock and expose it to the worst imaginable conditions and it will function as it did the first day you took it out of its box. One of my Glocks has hundreds of thousands of rounds through it and I've never had to replace a thing, not even a spring. I've been around firearms for years and years and there's simply no other handgun with such a degree of consistent dependability, not matter what you can throw its way. Those $5,000 Wilsons, I've seen them consistently fail like their more reasonably priced base model 1911 cousins, because of dust, sand, moisture, you know the real-world, where you'll be fighting. Glock is the AK of Combat Handguns, they're nearly indestructible, their inexpensive and they always work.

It's like the iPhone. If given a choice and the cost was the same, would you choose the iPhone 1 or the iPhone 6? How about if I told you the iPhone 6 was actually less expensive, because that's the case for Glock. Since the Glock has less parts and its parts are made up from less expansive martial, they cost less. Since its creation nearly every major handgun manufacture has come up with their own versions to stay competitive. Some are decent alternatives; however, others are a complete waste of money.

The key when deciding on an alternate option, is to make sure it's as straightforward and isn't plagued by dangerous de-cocking buttons and catches and if at all possible doesn't have useless safeties.

If my life depended on it and all I had was a handgun, it would be a Glock 17. I'm not the only one. Since the 9-11 Attacks, our military has been exposed to up-close gunfights like never before, requiring the use have handguns. No more so than our courageous Special Operations units. Since that time, they too have begun to make the shift to the superiority and simplicity of the most practical handgun around. Check out the handgun being worn on the vest of the SEAL Team 6 Operator. Yes, that's right it's a Glock. These tactical professionals know, what matters most is NOT about taking the sexiest, coolest looking gun into battle, it's about the ability of accurately placing multiple rounds into their Threat in the shortest span of time, regardless of the circumstances, all the time, every time.

Multiplicity trumps size...

The second biggest controversy amongst avid firearms owners pertains to caliber choice. The argument can easily be condensed to the concept of 'Stopping Power'; a bullet or round's ability to 'Stop' a person dead in their tracks. So does caliber size actually make a difference? To a certain extent, caliber size does have a measured

effect downrange. Obviously a 20mm HE round can do tons more damage than a tiny BB pellet and 45 caliber projectile makes a bigger hole down range. However, simply because a particular round is bigger, doesn't mean it's better. When it relates to handgun battles, bigger is often worse. Tactically, the main objective of the handgun during a up close and personal fight, is to achieve as many hits on Threat in the shortest of time spans. It boils down to controllability due to the effects of recoil. In a fight, the more controllable a particular handgun is, the the less time it takes to accurately send another round. Yet, there is a point at which a particular caliber is simply too small to achieve the needed terminal damage down range. So the objective is to find that round which offers the most controllability, while still achieving adequate damage on your Threat.

The confusion has to do with a lack of understanding of the relationship between the dynamics of gunfights and its effect on ballistics as a whole. Too often people focus too heavily on 'Terminal Ballistics' which is only one component to the overall equation. Terminal Ballistics is the study of a given round's effect on the body itself to determine how fatal a particular round may be on impact. Obviously it's important to know the potential damage a particular round is capable of down range. The problem arises when people use Ballistics Gelatin tests, as means of determining fact and foretelling future.

Ballistics Gel is gel-like substance, which usually consist of a large rectangular cube, having the consistency of human flesh. The gelatin cube is typically about 10" x 10" x 20" and essentially becomes translucent bullet trap. It basically allows a person to see a bullet's performance through human like tissue. This would include its expansion upon impact, separation, wound cavity, trajectory and overall depth of penetration through simulated flesh. While ballistics gelatin is a great tool, it is also horribly deceiving. It leads people to assume conclusions, which simply can't be made with such limited scope of measurement.

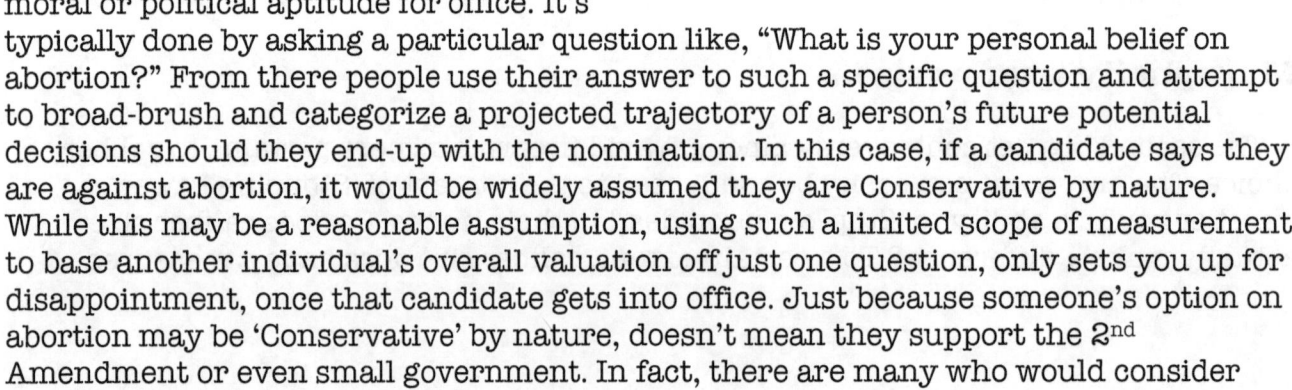

I liken Ballistic Gelatin tests to political Litmus tests. The Litmus test is method people use to determine a particular candidate's moral or political aptitude for office. It's typically done by asking a particular question like, "What is your personal belief on abortion?" From there people use their answer to such a specific question and attempt to broad-brush and categorize a projected trajectory of a person's future potential decisions should they end-up with the nomination. In this case, if a candidate says they are against abortion, it would be widely assumed they are Conservative by nature. While this may be a reasonable assumption, using such a limited scope of measurement to base another individual's overall valuation off just one question, only sets you up for disappointment, once that candidate gets into office. Just because someone's option on abortion may be 'Conservative' by nature, doesn't mean they support the 2nd Amendment or even small government. In fact, there are many who would consider themselves 'Liberal' leaning, who do not support abortion as well. While a Litmus test may be useful in narrowing down a person's personal options, they are NOT some sort of fail proof crystal ball capable of predicting future outcomes.

What Ballistic Gelatin can NOT do, is evaluate terminal performance so as to articulate an overall valuation of effect, on the actual dynamics of a given fight itself. What this means is, a cube of 'Simulated' flesh, can't tell you how, chemicals and hormones like adrenalin, dopamine and say testosterone, effect a particular round's overall stopping capability. Nor can Ballistic Gelatin tests, speak to all the other factors associated with an actual fight against a violently attacking Threat. Just because a particular round appears to have devastating effects on simulated flesh, doesn't mean that round; in and of itself, has the ability to prevent a Threat from fighting 'Through' the pain, in spite of even a the most devastating wound.

A good example of this occurs all the time in forests across the world. Any experienced hunter could tell you that just because you shoot an animal in its heart and literally blow it apart with a rifle round, doesn't mean the animal will drop. In fact, deer and other animals can run for 5-minutes after such a devastating blow, especially if they're in the Rut and high on adrenalin and testosterone. Why, because there is a difference between the simple Cause of Death and the actual State of Being Dead. While a particular wound may be the actual Cause which brought death, in a gunfight, death most usually comes after the body has drained itself of blood. Similarly, a Red Stag in the Rut, could be shot though its heart and still be able to run a mile or more, before the 'Loss of Blood' shuts its body down, finally causing it to falls to its death.

What people so often assume, is that simply because the .45 ACP consistently shows a far bigger wound cavity than the 9mm Luger, that the .45 ACP must me a deadlier round. While I'll agree that (1) .45 ACP round may cause a more mortally fatal wound than the 9mm Luger, in an actual fight, the 9mm Luger is far more capable of being the more 'Deadly' option if applied correctly.

In the real-world, in real gunfights, especially when handguns are used, what stops a Threat is not how big the hole is but rather a particular round's Blood Loss Potential. Once the body's blood volume diminishes bellow a particular level, the body then becomes inoperable. It's when a body reaches this state of being, where the superhuman effects of adrenaline meet their match. When considering wound valuation at its most simplistic form, it's obvious that a bigger hole makes for a bloodier wound, so the bigger wound must mean the bigger round has a higher Blood Loss Potential. However, it's not that simple. To determine Blood Loss Potential, you must take into account a given round's Follow-up Rate. The concept of a given firearm's Follow-up Rate, has to do with how quickly the shooter is able to get back on Threat after recoil, for an 'Accurate' follow-up shot. So the mathematical expression for determining Blood Loss Potential, looks more like a trigonometry function as opposed to basic addition and subtraction.

Let's just say a .45 ACP has a wound cavity of 2-inches in diameter, where as a 9mm Luger only has a 1.5-inch diameter wound cavity. If the simple severity of the wound is what's used to determine how deadly that wound is, and if the valuation is based off a

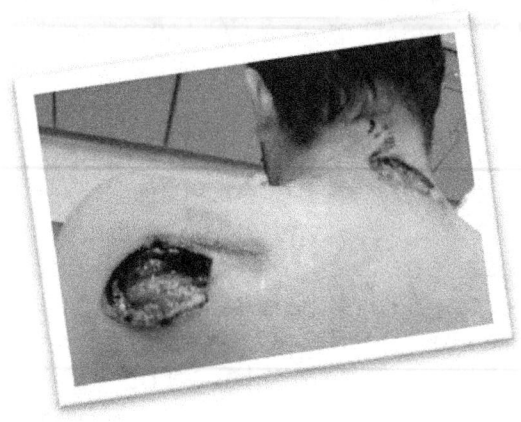

number, then it's a simple comparison of the difference between wound cavities. So subtracting the difference would tell you the .45 ACP is the winner by half an inch.

However, when considering the effect that the dynamics of the fight has on the Threat's ability to fight through devastating wounds, you soon realize the math becomes a bit more involved. When a Threat's blood is flooded with chemicals and hormones, its effect gives them an almost superhuman-like ability to overcome injury and prolong the fight. Because of this reality, multiplicity of shots becomes an important factor and so we have to infuse a calculation for Follow-up Rate. Since we're comparing the 45ACP to the 9mm Luger, let's use the Glock 21 (45 ACP) and the Glock 17 (9mm) as our controls.

Since the 9mm Luger's recoil is less abrupt than the 45 ACP, it takes a Glock 17 shooter less time to accurately send their next follow-up shot. Studies have shown this to be around 1.5 times that of the 45 ACP. So with these numbers a more realistic equation for how 'Deadly' these rounds are, would look like this:

Blood Loss Potential

Follow-up Rate^2 x Wound Cavity = Blood Loss Potential

or

$FR^2 * WC = BLP$

Glock 21 (45ACP)
Follow-up Rate: 4 Rounds-Per Second
Wound Cavity: 2-inches
Score: 32 BLP

Glock 17 (9mm Luger)
Follow-up Rate: 6 Rounds-Per-Second
Wound Cavity: 1.5-inches
Score: 54 BLP

You'll notice something quite different about this equation, in that you're going to 'Square' the Follow-up Rate. The reason for this is to valuate the Shock Effect each additional round has to the Threat's Central Nervous System. It's this important factor that's so often overlooked.

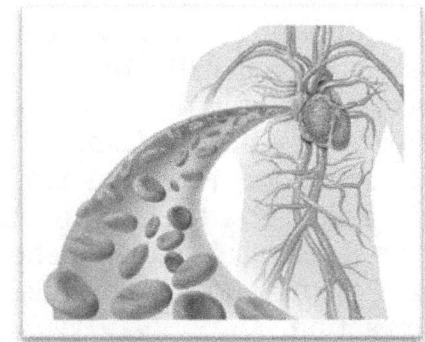

You see adrenaline and dopamine have and overriding effect on the Central Nervous System's electrical currents which run to your brain. When injury occurs, the nerves in that area scream out for help. That scream is echoed along an electrical current from the injury location to the brain and back. The body is designed to protect itself and maintain body function. So when your brain translates the scream into injury, it sends that message to the remainder of the body. What happens is the brain forces the body into a lower state much overall function. It then isolates the affected area, then goes about protecting that area from further damage, by intensifying the pain respecters of the nerves in that particular region. So when you break your leg, the brain tells the rest of the body to compensate, while also telling the affected leg to send excruciatingly sharp pain through the leg, if you attempt to bear weight on it. It's the 'Pain' which cause you to stop walking, thereby preventing further injury to that leg.

However, when adrenaline and other toxic chemicals and hormones are introduced, they override the body's pain mechanism. Giving you an ability to walk on a broken leg without feeling the as much pain. The more adrenalinly charged your Threat's blood is, the less pain he will feel. The less pain he feels, the less effect a particular injury has in its immediacy. To counteract the effects of adrenalin, you must increase the rate of damage on the system, or in other words, your rate-of-fire.

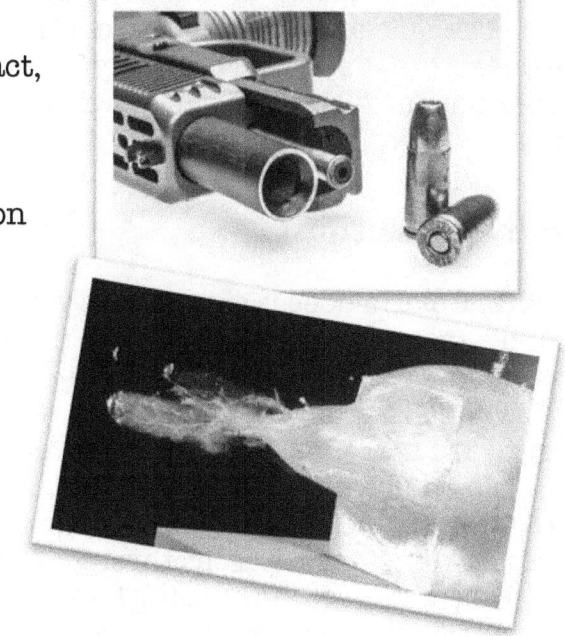

Here's why. There are countless stories of people being mortally wounded, yet still being capable of fighting in spite of their injuries. In fact, there are even cases where the Threat actually wins the fight 'After' being fatally shot. How's that? In these cases, the Threat receives a fatal wound, but continues to fight and kills the person who gave them that wound and then the Threat finally succumbs to his wound and also dies. It happens all the time for the very same reason a deer who's been shot, is capable of running a mile before they eventually fall and die.

For instance, I investigated a case where a suicidal lady killed herself approximately 2 ½ minutes after a Deputy literally blew her heart apart with a 1oz shotgun slug. She was able to keep shooting at the Deputies, sustaining (3) more gunshot wounds, until her body shutdown finally shutdown. At that point she collapsed to her back, shot herself (3) times in the chest and (2) times in the face, with the last shot to the face being ruled as the actual Cause of Death. What's interesting about this case, is that had she been wheeled into surgery immediately following the fatal shot to her heart, she would have still died.

The moral of the story comes down to the required need for immediately, massive blood loss. She stopped fighting only once her body had drained its self of the required supply of blood she needed to continue the fight.

If a gunfight, the objective is not Wound Size but rather Wound Effect. Your mission is to overload the Central Nervous System to such a degree, that it causes the other body's systems to go into Meltdown Mode and you must achieve this as quickly as possible. Meltdown Mode is most quickly achieved, through the multiplicity of wound infliction, within an extremely small time frame. In other words, the quicker you fill your Threat with 'Multiple' holes, the sooner he'll fall. It's the multiplicity of the infliction, which has the greatest overall effect.

Increasing your rate-of-fire, by sending multiple rounds into your Threats body in a short time span; one right after the other, gives each consecutive round an even greater Wound Potential than the one before it, thereby maximizing overall Wound Effect. The greater the 'Effect' a particular wound has on the body; the more overall Shock Effect it has on the Central Nervous System. The Shock Effect from the hydrostatic pressure associated with the wound cavity, decreases blood clotting thereby significantly thinning the blood itself. At the same time, it increases blood pressure, while also sending the heart rate through the roof.

The combined effect, when you introduce the multiplicity of gunshot wounds, very quickly becomes catastrophic. It's this combined Wound Effect, who's value is squared with each consecutive round, which causes blood to poor from effected areas, thereby maximizing total blood loss. So when comparing the 45 ACP to a much smaller 9mm Luger, with the more realistic Blood Loss Potential rating just listed, the 9mm Luger is capable of a much greater degree of Wound Effect, making the 9mm Luger a much more 'Deadly' round.

What this all means is that in a gunfight, the application of fire is what counts the most. The quicker you're able to continue the application of accurate fire, the sooner the battle is won. It's the veracity of your shots which places your Threat's body into a state of meltdown. Weather they die or not, well that depends on where you make those holes.

Round Selection...

What Gelatin does is simulate a given round's trajectory through human flesh. It gives you a wound value to work with. Even if that wound is catastrophic, such as the 1oz shot to the heart mentioned earlier, the fight WILL go on unless you fire-for-effect. The goal is to find a round that provides efficient retained weight as it passes through flesh, while at the same time offering less recoil so as to allow for a higher rate-of-fire.

The top three most popular handgun rounds are the .45 ACP, 40 S&W and 9mm Luger. All three are equally fatal. Why do I say this? Well a shot to the heart with either one will usually result in death. You can't exactly be deader than dead, so if they're all capable of causing death, then they must be equally fatal. However, as mentioned previously, the 9mm Luger is a better fighting round, since it has a higher potential for blood loos. That's why the Special Operations Community has adopted the 9mm Luger over both the .45 ACP and 40 S&W. The answer why is because the 9mm Luger is more practically effective for tactical purposes. The 9mm Luger is:

- Cost effective
- Easy to acquire
- Easiest to shoot
- Far more accurate
- Can be shot at greater distances
- Proper balance of overall Ballistics

- Offers the shooter more overall rounds per magazine

The goal in a gunfight is to WIN. Winning requires you to fight smarter not harder. The biggest problem with the .45 ACP and 40 S&W pertains to the 'Extra' effort a shooter must employ in order accurately place multiple rounds on their intended Threat.

The .45 ACP has an extremely slow and long recoil. What this means is it takes a considerable amount of time for the handgun's axis to resettle, meaning any rounds fired before it levels, are much more likely to completely miss the Threat. This also means it's a harder round to shoot in quick succession. The .45 ACP is also a very slow moving round. In fact, most people can actually see the round flying through the air when shooting at distances of 25 meters or greater. Due to its slow muzzle velocity, it is completely impractical at ranges over 50 meters. Why would you want to shoot further than 50 meters? Parking lots at the mall or corridors and hallways of office buildings are far greater than 50 meters. During an Active Shooter / Active Threat situation, you may need to engage a Threat at extended ranges. The .45 ACP is a bigger round meaning it costs more to produce. The other sacrifice to size is that they take up more room in your magazine, meaning you're left with far less rounds-per-mag than the 9mm Luger.

The 40 S&W's is a very interesting round altogether. In all honesty it's a science project gone bad. You would think since is smaller than the .45 ACP, then it must have less recoil. Unfortunately, that's not the case. While the .45 ACP's recoil rates higher in foot-pounds of energy, the 40 S&W's recoil is far snappier. Basically the 40 S&W is a .45 ACP in a 9mm package, meaning its recoil and ballistics as a whole, are completely unbalanced. This mean's the .45 ACP actually has more manageable recoil. On top of this, the 40 S&W's snappiness, makes it far less accurate in quick succession than the .45 ACP. The 40 S&W is also bigger than the 9mm, so it costs more and leaves the shooter with less rounds-per-mag. If you were to poll the average professional shooter, you'd find an overwhelming hatred of the 40 S&W altogether. You'll also hear those same people say the only reason they shoot the 40 S&W is because it's the one their agency or company chose.

Self-Defense Ammo...

Another misunderstood factor with ammunition selection has to do with the composition of the actual projectile itself. There are two predominant types of bullet compositions, the Full Metal Jacket (FMJ) or the Hollow Point (HP). Due to the Geneva Convention's rules on bullet type, the FMJ is by far the most commonly used worldwide. Like is usually the case, popularity does NOT mean the FMJ is better. What's interesting is why the United Nations made this distinction in the first place.

In the eyes of the U.N., an HP bullet is 'Inhuman'. Why, because it inflicts devastating bodily harm. Upon impact with flesh, an HP bullet rapidly expands like a star and rips its way through flesh, bone, organs and creates a massive wound cavity and exit wound. An FMJ on the other hand, retains a majority of its overall shape, passes through flesh, like a hot knife to butter and leaves a far less devastating exit wound.

The U.N. is in the business of Peace Keeping; they don't want armies killing each other. So they require armies to use inferior weaponry like the FMJ. However, the act of Combat itself is not about keeping peace it's about 'Making' peace. When it comes to Self-Defense, the person defending themselves is defending against an attack on their very existence. In this situation, death is not a possibility but rather a high and likely probability. So, the person defending themselves needs to kill their Threat quickly, so as to afford themselves the best chances of survival. So in a gunfight, killing your Threat before he's able to kill you, is your most paramount important objective.

Ironically hunters have historically opted for HP bullets because they have a higher potential of death, thereby making them not only more practical, but far more humane. The hunting world has perfected the act of killing animals, so that its done with ease and with speed. In all reality, a gunfight is no different than a hunt. Your Threat is hunting you and you are hunting your Threat. The only difference is that the animal you hunt walks upright and shoots back. You need to kill your prey as quickly as entirely possible and bullet choice directly effects the outcome. Choosing the right bullet will assist in achieving this goal with expeditious finality. However, choosing the wrong bullet in a gunfight, will prolong the fight itself, make it harder for you to win and exponentially increases your chances of death. When it comes to Self-Defense you require Personal Defense ammunition or HP bullets. Save the less expensive FMJ's for practice.

Top 3 Full-Size Combat Handguns...

The Full-Size Combat Handgun is hands down your best suited option. It affords the most ammunition, adequate grip, extended barrel length and is typically the most comfortable size to shoot while under rapidly fire. It's also the easiest to retain during a struggle. However, they are larger and heavy handguns and not typically the best Concealed Carry gun. Here are my Top 3 Glock style full-size options you should really consider.

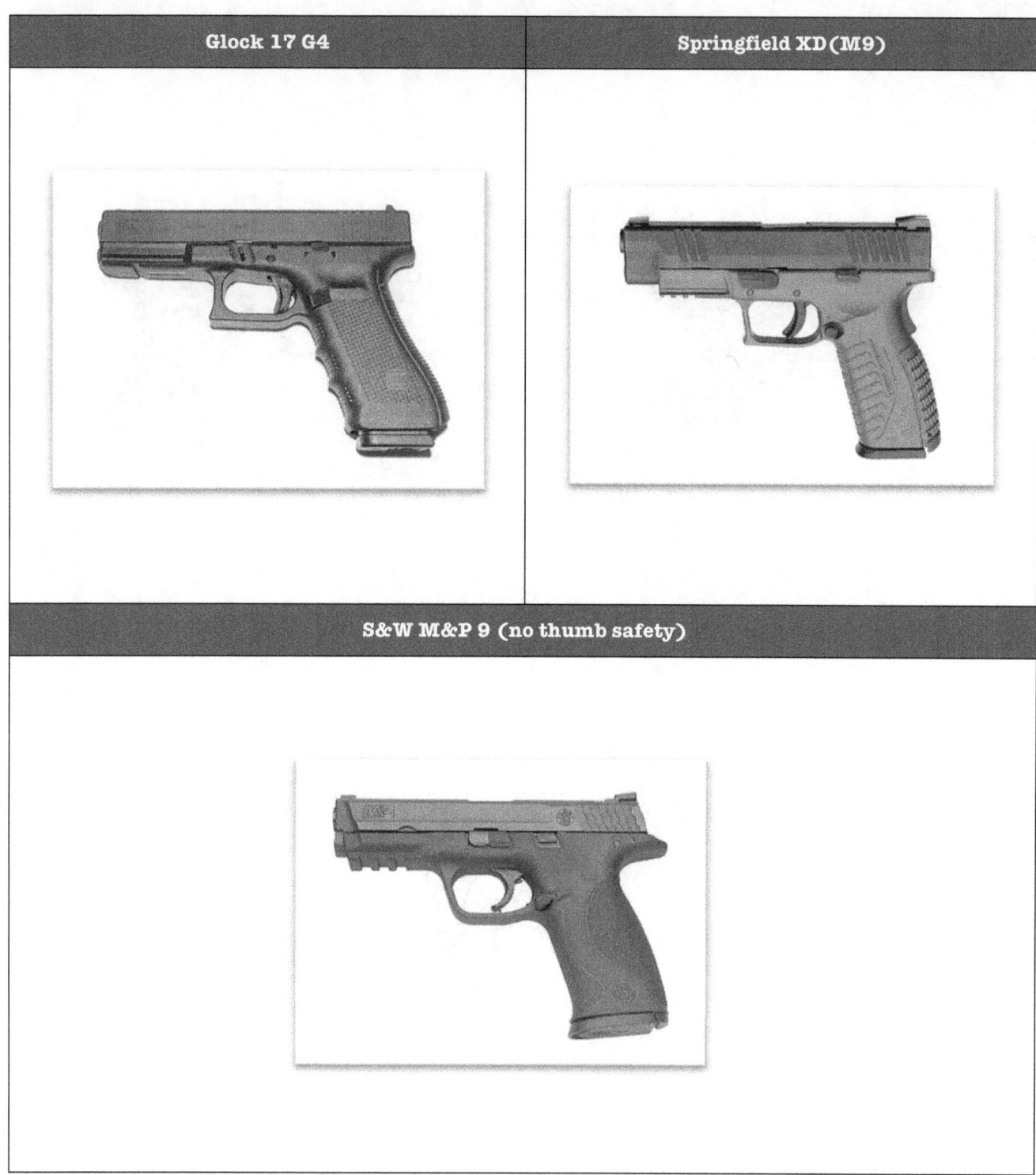

Top 3 Compact Combat Handguns...

The Compact Combat Handgun is your next best suited variant. It affords a decent balance of conceal ability, while still maintaining adequate ammunition, decent grip size and acceptable barrel length. While they are much easier to conceal than their Full-Size brothers, they are not as comfortable to shoot, especially for individuals with large hands. However, they fit a purpose and that is for the mission of conceal ability. Here are my Top 3 Glock style compact sized variants you should really consider.

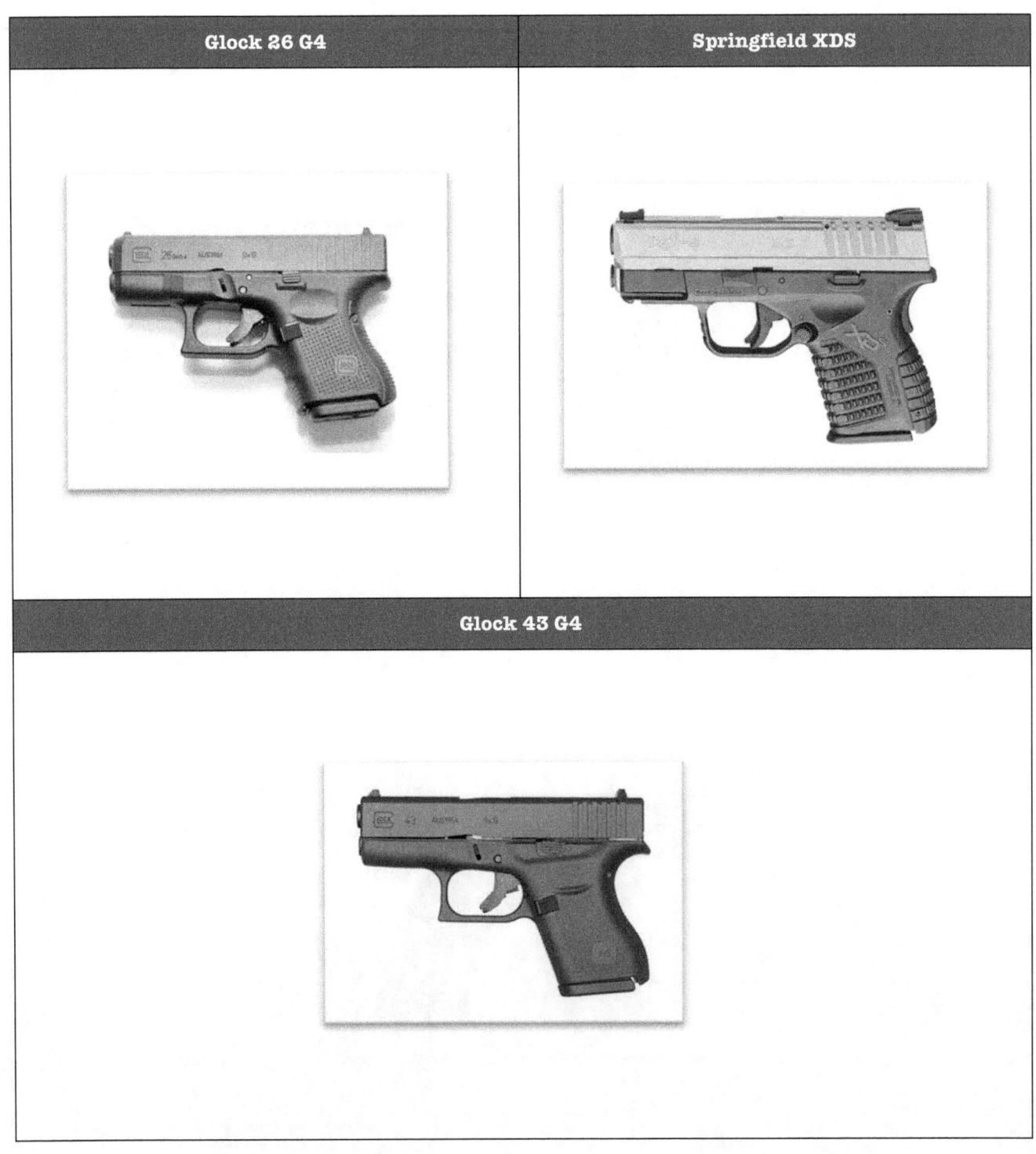

Top 3 Sub-Compact Combat Handguns...

The Sub-Compact Combat Handgun is your alternative for deep conceal ability. It affords the ability to easily carry a fighting style handgun with lightweight or formal attire, or even in a pocket. However, with such a scaled-down size, you will make some scarifies. These are by far the least comfortable to shoot, do not offer as many rounds and can be very finicky on ammunition. Yet they do serve their purpose and are your best alternative, when you require the greatest conceal ability. Here are my Top 3 Glock style sub-compact sized alternatives you should really consider.

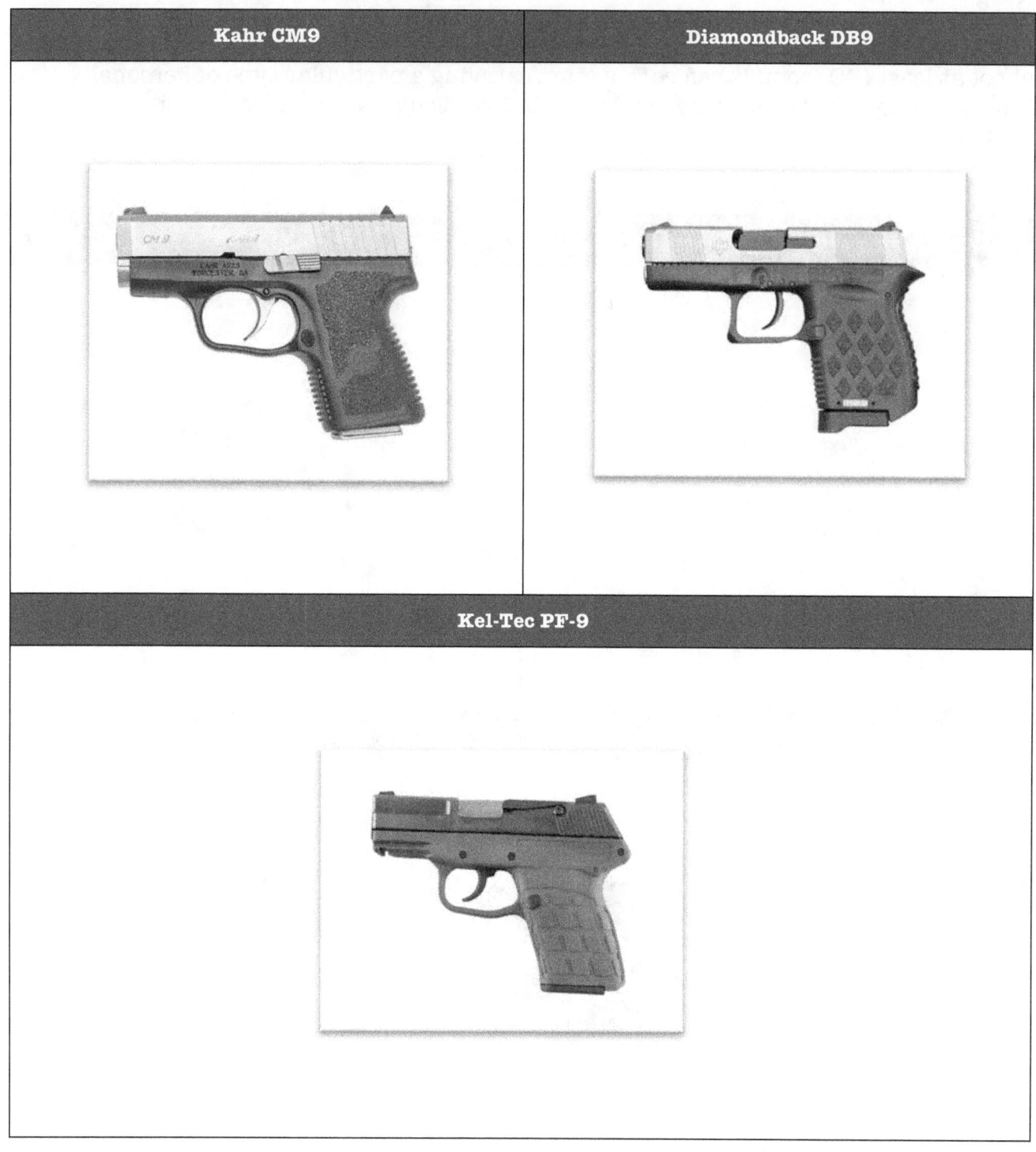

Top 3 Personal Defense Rounds...

There are dozens of ammunition manufactures around with hundreds of ammunition choices. It's important to understand that not all Personal Defense ammunition are created equal. When you go to war to save your life, you need to show up to that fight with the best ammunition capable of assisting in winning that fight. Cutting corners to for the least expensive box, is not a viable option. Doing so will increase the potential for firearms malfunctions during the fight, be less effective of actually killing your Threat and in turn, make the task of wining and surviving, a very difficult one. For this reason, I've selected three of the best Personal Defense rounds on the market and encourage you to fix your sights on one of these options. Keep in mind, Personal defense ammunition is expensive at about $1-2 a piece. You'll need to purchase enough to fill your main magazine and any spares you may carry. It's also important that you shoot at least (40) rounds before you start carrying a particular type of Personal Defense ammunition. This way you know that particular ammunition functions properly.

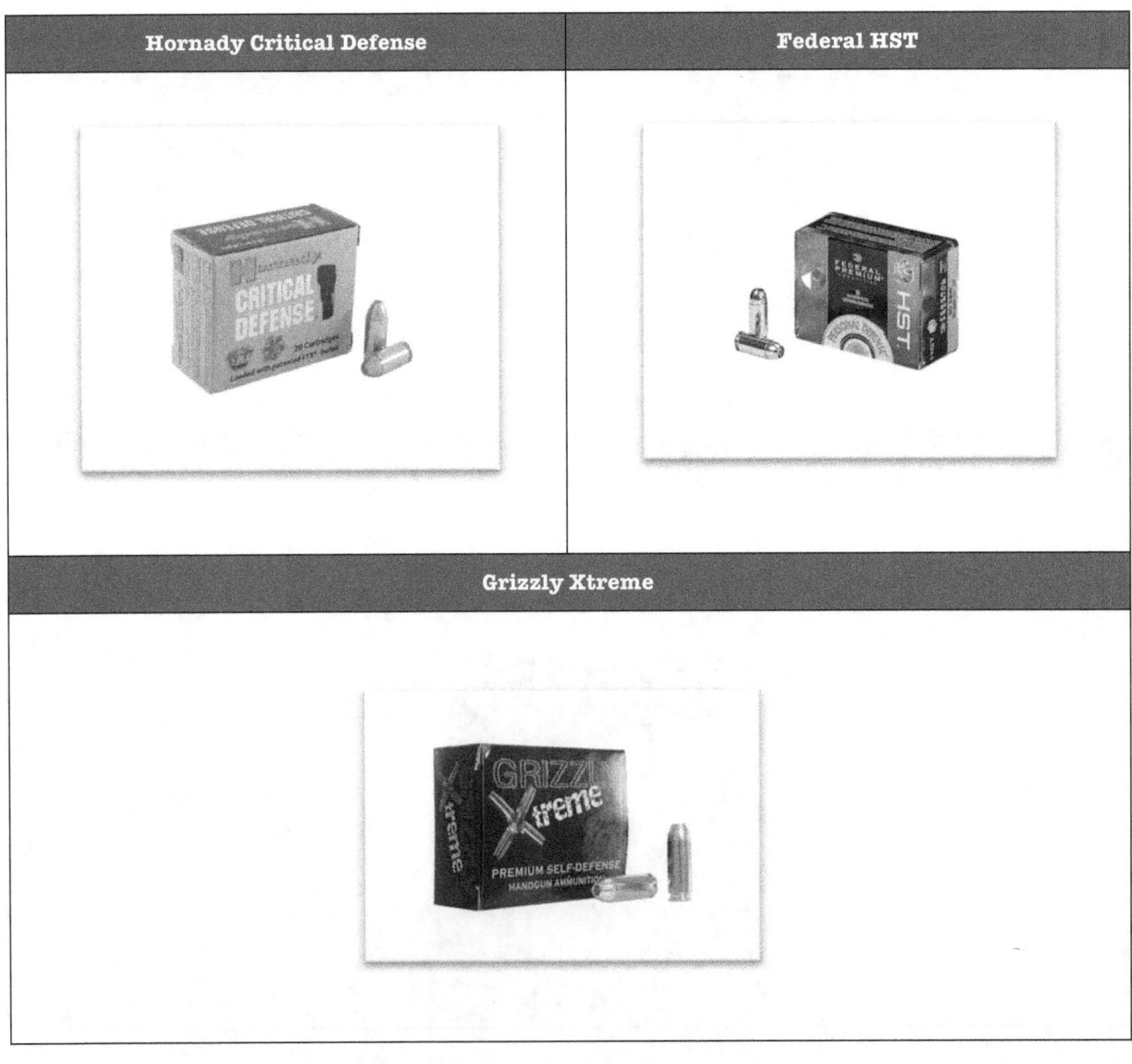

Top 3 FMJ Training Rounds...

When it's time to hit the range for training, you'll likely shoot dozens of rounds. If you're attending a training class, you may even shoot hundreds of rounds. Using Personal Defense ammunition for training could break your bank, since some Personal Defense rounds cost about $1-2 a piece. For this reason, you'll need to switch to a decent FMJ. There are dozens of ammunition manufactures who produce FMJ ammunition. The key is not to buy the cheapest option. The vast majority of lesser expensive ammunition, is made overseas and are NOT generally as safe. It's best to stick with proven manufactures who have a long safety record. It's also important to know that some handguns are very finicky, when it comes to FMJ ammunition. Since FMJ rounds are not produced to the same tolerances as Personal Defense ammunition, they have a tendency to cause malfunctions. So before you purchase in bulk, try a few boxes to assure they work well in your handgun. Here are three proven FMJ training options that operate superbly in most handguns.

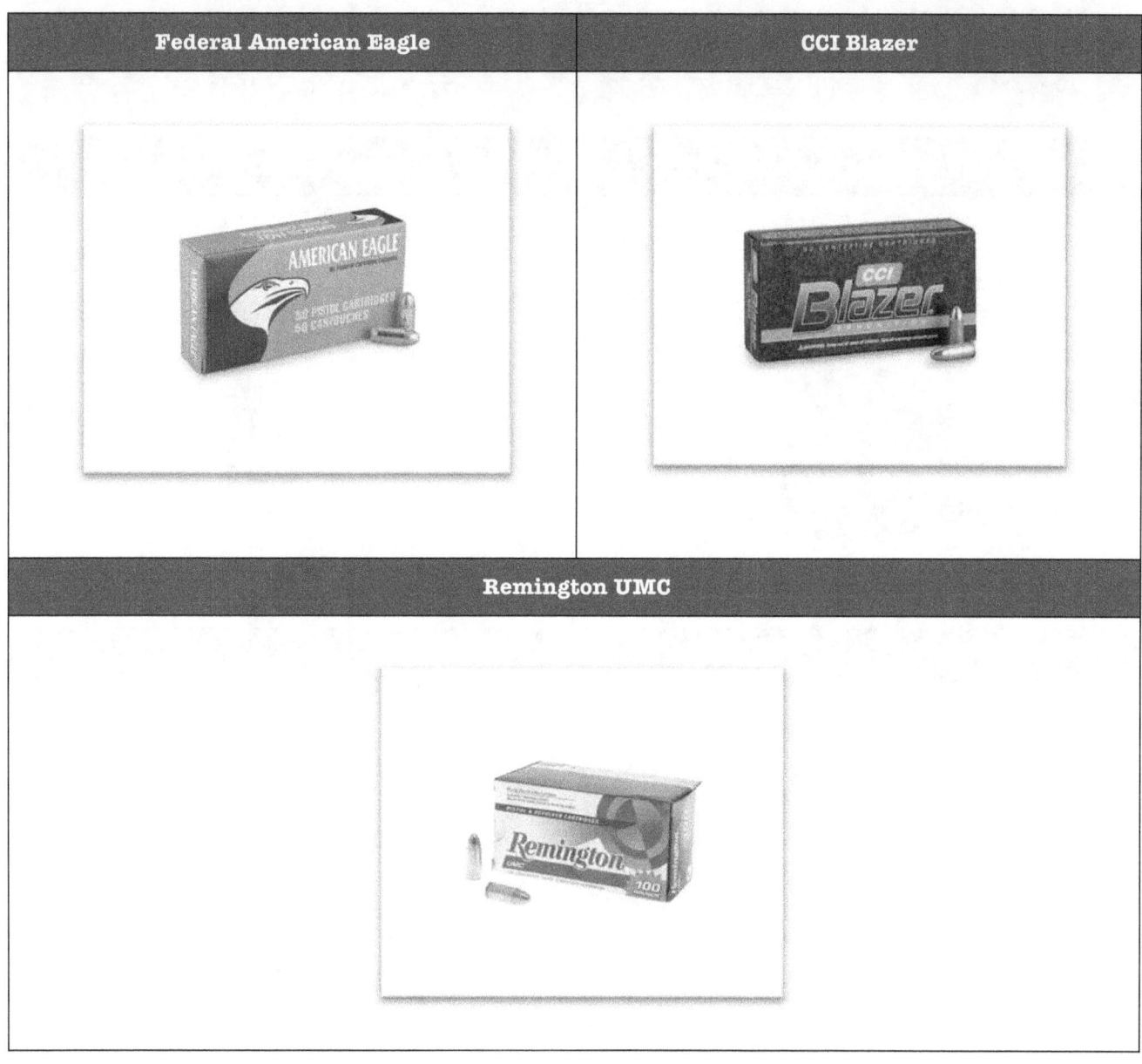

Top 3 Holsters...

Time is a commodity you do NOT have in a tactical environment. If you can't access your weapon and obtain a firm grip, you won't be able to fight with it. There are thousands of holster companies and tens of thousands of holsters out there. I have picked the following (3) for good reason.

When it comes to Concealed Carry, on the waist carry, is your most suitable option, with Inside the Waistband (IWB) being the most concealable. I have found the Alien Cloak Tuck 3.0 to be the most practical (IWB) holster in existence. There is a lot to be said about its versatility and adaptability, as well as being extremely affordable. It can also be adapted to an (OWB) rig.

Generally speaking, Outside the Waistband (OWB), carry is best suited for the range, duty and or tactical situations, as it does not provide ideal conceal ability. You should really consider the Blackhawk SERPA for (OWB) carry. The SERPA system is hands down the best tactical holster system in existence. It allows for multiple holster security level options, as well as a tactical light option. What takes the SERPA to a world of its own, is its ability to be used on multiple platforms from waist, vest, to drop-leg carry, via the SERPA Quick Disconnect Kit.

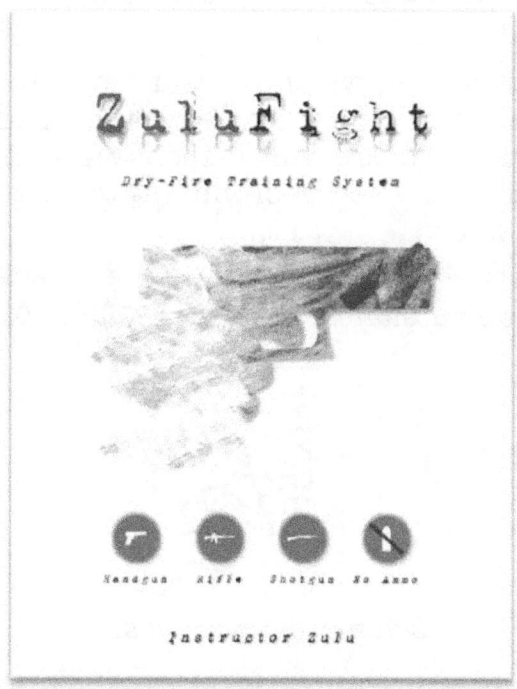

Whether you're a civilian or armed professional, this breakthrough system will take your firearms proficiency to an unthinkable level. With an exponential increase in random violent crime, deadly confrontations have become a new norm in nearly every community, from urban centers to the countryside.

Firearms Self-Defense is much for than accuracy on a range or high scores in competition. Face-to-face confrontations are the most fluidly dynamic environment you'll ever encounter. The realities and consequences associated with gunfights, often come at the highest costs. Sadly, the vast majority of training techniques are dangerous and useless at best, especially when attempted in real-life gunfights. Adding fuel to the fire, most so called 'Firearms Experts' endorse fatally impractical tactics, which attempt to defy the scientific realities of conflict itself.

ZuluFight is founded on the irrefutable physical parameters associated with deadly encounters. It utilizes the most scientifically recognized method of firearms training; Dry-Fire, enabling you an ability to encode perfect movement. But not all Dry-Fire methods are equal. The vast majority focus too heavily on only two aspects of shooting, the draw and trigger squeeze. ZuluFight masters the kinesis of shooting, turning Dry-Fire into a Kata. This allows you the capability of honing every single aspect of shooting. In fact, ZuluFight is a 'Total Training System' in that you're able to isolate and master each ingredient to a sound Fight Response, everything from:

- Start Positions, Stance, Presentation & Trigger Manipulation
- Reloads & Malfunction Mitigation
- Holsters & Slings
- After Action Tactical Awareness & Fight Psychology
- As well as all eight firearms fundamentals

Best of all, ZuluFight is specifically designed for handguns, rifles and even shotguns. It's cookbook format is straightforward and easy to follow. There's no re-occurring cost, no ammunition, no trips to the range and is achieved from the comforts of your own home.

The advantages of this lifesaving system, is your key to tomorrow's victory. ZuluFight will boost your accuracy more than any other method. You'll gain real proficiency, while exponentially decreasing response time, for an instantaneous kinesthetic response. Discover the secret of winning tomorrow's battle today. Train today so you're ready tomorrow!

Don't Hesitate. Perfect your Kata TODAY!

zulutactical.com/zulufight

Are you prepared for the all-encompassing legal battle you'll face, when you use Deadly Force? The most overlooked aspect of Self-Defense has to do with what comes after the incident.

The complicated and completely unavoidable obstacles, which immediately follow every use of Deadly Force, requires a very unique and preemptive strategy, if one hopes to come out unscathed. Sadly, most civilians and attorneys alike, save the planning for tomorrow. A sad reality is you can be completely justified, cleared of all Criminal wrongdoing and still be found liable in a Civilly proceeding. Meaning, it's completely possible to be stuck paying millions, for doing the right thing.

However, there are important, practical steps you can take today, to avoid tomorrow's legal onslaught. This step-by-step system is your preemptive approach, for an impenetrable legal defense. ZuluShield is a must have for anyone who may one day be forced to protect life with a firearm or even with their hands. Whether you're a private citizen or a seasoned police officer, ZuluShield is your solution to the most complicated legal problems.

Learn what you can do today and the vitally important things you must do directly following such an incident, to avoid a legal catastrophe. Get protected today, discover the secrets for a bulletproof Firearms Legal Defense. Prepare today so you're ready tomorrow!

Don't Hesitate. Get Protected TODAY!

zulutactical.com/zulushield

 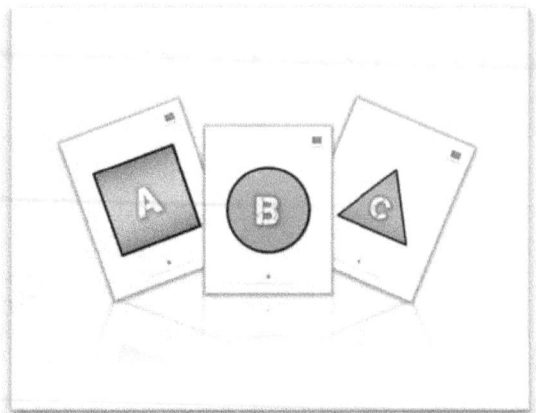

- Stay Aware & Stay Alive -

When it comes to deadly confrontations, one constant remains true, there is always a significant risk of like. Your survival is dependent upon your ability to remain Tactically Aware, even under the most extreme stress. It comes down to how well you're able to calculate the totality of the circumstances presented and employ a solution that's based on strategy. It's a calculative response, rather than one that's purely reactive by nature.

What are ABCs Tactical Awareness Aides?

ABCs Tactical Awareness Aides are scientifically based training aides, capable of actually conditioning a high state of Cognitive Awareness in high stress, fluid environments. ABCs placards are specifically designed to condition your brain's ability to multi-task with clarity, even under the most extreme levels of stress. ABCs are easy to use and can be included in almost any training environment, for a multitude of functions.

ABCs Tactical Awareness Aides packages include:

- Highly visible
- Durable & waterproof
- Easily fastened or held
- 9 full-color laminated placards
- 18 combinations of colors, shapes & letters

Here's how they work:

Situational Awareness is the Cognitive Association with one's environment. However, Tactical Awareness the ability to remain Situationally Aware, during times of extreme stress, such as deadly confrontations.

The dilemma, is that Tactical Awareness is a state-of-mind. It's not a tangible skillset like shooting, making it a difficult thing to master. It's a process of continually identifying and relating with your environment, with a very high degree of cognition. However, science tells us cognitive function exponentially diminishes as stress levels increase. So developing a habit of Tactical Awareness, requires a very unique scientific approach, that's achieved through repetition.

ABCs Tactical Awareness Aides are an ingenious and simple way to achieve this, because they use kindergarten level brain development techniques, as a means of giving your brain an ability to 'Think' under stress.

When it comes to Firearms Self-Defense, one of the most widely practiced techniques and an attempt at conditioning Tactical Awareness, is the 'After Action Scan.' Basically, the shooter scans their environment; left and right, after the course of fire, so as to seek for possible hazards and threats or places of potential cover. However, what's missing on nearly every range is the 'Seeking' element. Most After Action Scans become a mere physical turn of one's head, a glance and a look. In order to actually 'Seek', you've gotta have something to seek, as well as a particular level of Active Thought. You need to actually see something and identify it, thereby giving it a value in relation to other objects in its environment.

To correctly condition Tactical Awareness, you have to go about including repetitively Cognitive Association drills in training, which activate four important brain functions:

- Visual
- Associative
- Intellectual
- Verbal

Including ABCs placards in your training regime, makes this a simple process. In Kindergarten our vocabulary was founded on the building blocks of the ABCs. Likewise, ABCs placards, give you an ability to sustain Cognitive Association, by conditioning your brain to continually identify and associate,

- Color
- Shape
- Name

While this may appear elementary, be assured, the task becomes difficult when combining it with some type of kinesthetic function like shooting i.e. After Action Scan. What it does is force the brain to multi-task,

- Visually (see the object)
- Associatively (identify its composition)
- Intellectually (associate & differentiate its qualities)
- Verbally (communicate its value)

Each time the user identifies and values an ABCs placard, they've completed a very important back-and-forth conversation of sorts, with the left and right hemispheres of the brain. Overtime, the task becomes easier, thereby honing the user's comprehensive decision making through Active Thought.

How can ABCs Tactical Awareness Aides be used?

ABC's are extremely multi-faceted and can be used in a number of different training environments. The idea is to condition practical and fluid awareness. So, for skills which require divided attention ABCs will take that ability to a whole new level.

Firearms Self-Defense:

ABCs placards can be used to aide with After Action Scans or even placed on or near targets to assist in training Threat ID & Association.

Reconnaissance & Surveillance Training:

ABCs placards can be positioned in various places in the training environment to help gage and test a trainee's level of awareness and attention to detail.

Tactical Operations Training:

ABCs placards can be positioned throughout a building during entry drills, forcing members of the Entry element to visual and verbally identify ABC's as they pass through the structure, forcing them to multi-task at speed and under stress.

Emergency Vehicle Operation Training:

Anyone who's worked as a First Responder, knows the stress and dynamics of simply driving to the scene. ABC's placards can take EVOC to a whole new level and help condition a trainee to multi-task visually and verbally while also completing the other multitude of functions while driving.

Those are just a few of the many ways ABCs Tactical Awareness Aides can be used. How you'll use them depends on your imagination. Think outside the box and make your training the best training possible. Take your training to the next level. Gaining Tactical Awareness is as easy as the ABCs.

Don't Hesitate. Stay Aware TODAY!

zulutactical.com/abcs

ZuluWarrior Training Group:

Are you ready to experience the most repeatable, realistic and reliable firearms training program giving you the most practical solution for tomorrow's deadly encounter? Are you ready to learn realistic tactics so you can play Tactical Chess while your threat plays Checkers? Use the QR Code to the right or visit our website today!

zulutactical.com/training

TeamZulu:

Stay up to date with all things *ZULU*. Connect with us on Facebook. Learn why fans from around the World choose *ZULU*. Use the QR Code to the right or visit our website today!

facebook.com/zulutac

Armed Private Security Officer WRITTEN EXAM

The four Cardinals Firearms Safety Rules are: (write out the complete sentence or phrase)

1. _____
   _____
   _____

2. _____
   _____
   _____

3. _____
   _____
   _____

4. _____
   _____
   _____

5. It is always your personal_____to ensure the safety of yourself and others any time you handle a firearm.

6. If you shoot another person accidentally, you may be charged with a crime.

                                                                    TRUE   FALSE

7. No firearm should be left unattended.

                                                                     TRUE   FALSE

8. A firearm in your home should be stored unloaded, under lock and accessible only to trained, responsible persons.

                                                                     TRUE   FALSE

9. Before you accept the responsibility of carrying a gun as an armed private security officer, you are required to decide if you are willing to shoot, and if

necessary kill, if the situation demands it.

                                                                 TRUE   FALSE

10. As a private security officer you have NO duty to act when confronted with unlawful behavior or resistance. Instead of taking direct action you may decide to observe and report criminal behavior rather than attempt to arrest, detain or use force.

                                                                 TRUE   FALSE

11. "Physical force that under the circumstances in which it is used is readily capable of causing death or serious physical injury" is the definition of:

    a. Self defense
    b. Deadly physical force
    c. Serious physical injury
    d. Reasonable belief

12. Serious Physical Injury as defined by ORS 161.015(8) means physical injury which creates a substantial risk of death.

                                                                 TRUE   FALSE

13. Oregon law allows you to use deadly physical force to defend your life, but not the life of another person.

                                                                 TRUE   FALSE

14. You may not shoot a person who is running away from you, or who is attempting to steal or destroy property, or who is disobeying an order, and is NOT an immediate deadly threat.

                                                                 TRUE   FALSE

15. You become the_____when you use force that is not justified in the first place, or you continue to use force after there is no longer a need.

16. The armed private security officer can avoid using excessive force by:

    a. Knowing when it is lawful and proper to use force.
    b. Considering and, if possible, using alternatives to force.
    c. Using only the degree of force necessary to stop the attack or control the threat.
    d. Reducing the level of force if the threat stops using force, retreats or surrenders.
    e. All of the above.

17. An armed private security officer is never required to use force.

    TRUE   FALSE

18. Even if you are justified in using deadly physical force to defend your life, you may be prosecuted if you injure or kill innocent persons.

    TRUE   FALSE

19. In order to justify the use of deadly physical force three requirements must be met and exist together at the same point in time. These requirements are:

    a. Action, Reaction and De-escalation.
    b. Facts, Information and Experience.
    c. Means, Opportunity and Intent.

20. After using deadly physical force, you are required by law to talk to the police before you have an opportunity to obtain legal advice.

    TRUE   FALSE

21. What is the first recommended post-shooting action?

    a. Holster your weapon
    b. Get behind cover and observe that the threat is no longer a danger
    c. Notify law enforcement
    d. summon medical assistance and administer first aid within your training and ability

22. A concealed handgun License (CHL) allows a certified private security professional to be armed while on duty.

    TRUE   FALSE

23. When confronting a possible threat, you should identify yourself and give verbal commands that are _____ AND _____.

24. Even if you are justified in using deadly force to defend yourself or another person, you and your employer may be sued for damages by the person or the family of the person you used force against.

    TRUE   FALSE

25. Cover from gunfire is defined as any object that will stop a bullet.

    TRUE   FALSE

26. The interior and exterior walls of residential construction (dwelling) will usually not stop a handgun bullet.

    TRUE   FALSE

27. You do not gain a tactical advantage by keeping distance between you and the threat.

    TRUE   FALSE

28. The primary reason for the care and cleaning of the duty handgun is to ensure that it will fire when and if it is needed to protect the officer's life.

    TRUE   FALSE

29. Generally, warning shots are effective and highly recommended.

    TRUE   FALSE

30. Shooting at a person you have not identified as a deadly threat is permissible in low light conditions.

    TRUE   FALSE

Revised 11 2013

www.ingramcontent.com/pod-product-compliance
Lightning Source LLC
Chambersburg PA
CBHW080655190526
45169CB00006B/2133